SEGMENTING

THE MATURE MARKET

Identifying, targeting
and reaching America's
diverse, booming
senior markets

Based on the 50+® Studies

CAROL M. MORGAN
DORAN J. LEVY, Ph.D.

PROBUS PUBLISHING COMPANY
Chicago, Illinois
Cambridge, England

ISBN 1-55738-448-7

Printed in the United States of America

BB

1   2   3   4   5   6   7   8   9   0

TAQ/BJS

To the memory of Dora Rebolledo and Helen Fine Rosenberg.

TABLE OF CONTENTS

Part One — A New View of the Mature Market

ONE
Attitudes: What Drives the Market?   3

Understanding the consumer
Types of segmentation
What motivates mature consumers?
Our research process
Conclusion

TWO
Ways of Segmenting the Market   11

Attempts to categorize mature consumers
Demographic segmentation
Lifestyle segmentation
Retirement segmentation
Psychographic segmentation
Segmenting by media usage
Conclusion

THREE
The Importance of the Mature Market   21

A growing market
The mature as consumers, employees
Some (bad) reasons for avoiding this market
New way of thinking
Conclusion

Part Two — The Self Segments: Attitudes toward Life, Aging, and Finances

Part Three — The Health Segments: Views on Prevention and Sickness

Part Four — The Food Segments: Attitudes toward Eating and Nutrition

LIST OF FIGURES

ACKNOWLEDGMENTS

Completing this book was immensely facilitated by the persistence, organizing talents, proofing skills, patience, and intelligent suggestions of Suzanne Reinke. We will always be indebted to her commitment to the long process of seeing this book into print.

We also thank Edward Morgan for his work in data processing, producing run after run of data as we endeavored to better understand the segments.

The graphs that add so much to the visual appeal of this book were composed by John Morgan, who also worked on many small jobs related to this book, contributing to the overall whole.

Thanks too to Aaron Osterby and Bob Farrell for their contributions in proofing the manuscript.

Suggestions from Stephen W. Plumb and Joy McComb added much to the sense and readability of this work. Steve also contributed considerably to the precision and detail of the index which accompanies this book. Our thanks to Janice Shimokubo, our long-time friend and supporter, many of whose suggestions we incorporated.

We extend our heartfelt appreciation to Marsha Lindsay, President of Lindsay Stone & Briggs, for her comments on the book as it took shape. We were encouraged in writing the book by her progressive advertising agency's innovative marketing philosophy.

Although the original 1989 50+ study was self-funded, we appreciate the participation of several corporate sponsors in the 1991-92 syndicated study.

Finally, we wish to recognize the late Dr. William Stephenson, whose lifework had a profound influence on our effort to better understand the mature market.

PART ONE

A NEW VIEW OF THE MATURE MARKET

ONE

ATTITUDES: WHAT DRIVES THE MARKET?

"Marketers' attempts at reaching those over 50 have been miserably unsuccessful. No market's motivations and needs are so poorly understood. A new way of segmenting those over 50 based on their underlying motivating factors is desperately needed," says Peter Francese, publisher of *American Demographics*.

In response to the need that Francese expresses, we researched more than 3,600 persons over 50 between 1989 and 1992 and analyzed their needs and motivations. The proprietary methodologies we used are those we apply in our business for custom segmentation studies. From our large, quantifiable studies of the over-50 market, we developed three separate segmentation strategies.

These strategies present a unique perspective on the motivations of those over 50. The three 50+® segmentations are specific to perceptions on the self, aging, and finances; health; and food. To the best of our knowledge, no other examples exist of a multiple segmentation strategy on any single population.

Unlike global segmentations that are too general to be of much use, the 50+ segments are sufficiently specific to apply to scores of products and services. By examining persons over 50 in three different ways, we have simplified this complex market but have provided enough detail to give marketing and public policy planners clear direction.

In this chapter and the two that follow, we detail the failure of mass marketing in reaching the mature consumer and the need for a niche strategy. We describe why and how we developed the three 50+ segmentations and show how they can benefit those trying to reach the mature market. Various other segmentation approaches are analyzed, and we outline why they have provided only partial answers. Finally, in Chapter 3 we describe the possibilities and rewards that exist within the mature market.

We begin our analysis with the fundamental assertion of the mature market's diversity and show why mass marketing has failed in reaching mature consumers.

UNDERSTANDING THE CONSUMER

"It's a scary thought," the marketing director confided to us. "The marketing manager on our estrogen replacement drug for menopausal women is a 29-year-old bachelor."

Even if the marketing manager had a middle-aged mother, it is unlikely he could visualize the rich diversity of all of the lifestyles of people in this category. Large markets such as families with young children and people over 50 are not homogeneous. To make any sense of them at all, such markets must be divided into submarkets. Marketing managers must understand what motivates consumers within these submarkets to buy their products, or they will be doomed to inefficiency and failure.

Mass marketing

However, many marketers subscribe to the "cast the widest net" school of marketing. This view contends that different advertising campaigns, channels of distribution, and product lines for submarkets are impractical. Since they assume money is available for only one advertising strategy or want to keep production simple, these marketers survey their markets to find dominant, overarching themes for why consumers would buy their products.

This mass market strategy, while simple to manage, often results in large losses of opportunity. If several competitors take this point of view, they are likely to come up with the same general strategy. In such a case, they either fail to differentiate their products or depend on advertising themes to create a difference based on image. Often, since consumers find no meaningful differences among products, the fight for share among these brands is reduced to price-cutting.

"They can have any color, as long as it is black." This expression, attributed to Henry Ford, captures another aspect of the mass-market mentality, one that was probably more reasonable when mass production of automobiles was in its infancy. Detroit's unwillingness to expand its lines of automobiles to include compacts and front-wheel-drive models was, in turn, a major factor in the Japanese grabbing a large share of the American car market.

Theodore Levitt states that "early decline and certain death are the fate of companies whose policies are geared totally and obsessively to their own convenience at the total expense of the customer." We maintain that mass marketing is a convenience to marketers which necessarily produces an expense to consumers. Market segments with special needs are forced to compromise on products and services when marketers don't respond to their needs.

Diversification as reaction

At times, corporations do broaden their lines and diversify to satisfy different segments of their markets, but more often than not they are reactive rather than proactive. Why did a few young entrepreneurs start the wine cooler business on a shoestring, instead of at one of the big wine producers? Why was it possible for Steve Jobs and Steve Wozniak to start Apple Computer from a garage, instead of within the folds of IBM? It's evident now that IBM will pay a high price for being unresponsive to change.

Lists of small entrepreneurs challenging big business would cover many pages. The point is clear, however. The way to challenge a large share leader is to produce higher quality, more functionally specialized, or more distinctive products than a "one-size-fits-all" mass-market product. Mass marketers are being forced by competitors, changing technologies, regional differences, government regulations, new channels of distribution, international markets, and splintering media to diversify or die.

Niche marketing

Many marketers take views opposing the mass-market model. They believe their buyers are likely to differ from each other in many respects. By understanding the critical differences among interested consumers, these marketers focus their resources more effectively and better differentiate themselves from their competition.

The segmentation or niche market model is more efficient than the mass-market model for several reasons. First of all, niche market products or services are designed with a specific group of consumers in mind. Their designs require tight specifications to ensure customer satisfaction and long-lasting customer loyalty. Secondly, advertising messages can be crafted to deliver meaningful promises. The messages then are sent through carefully selected media to consumers known to be interested. Clearly, the days of a small number of buyers supporting the cost of communicating with a large number of nonbuyers are fast coming to a close.

This niche point of view is just as valid for government, charities, and other public entities as it is for the commercial marketing of goods and services. A niche perspective leads to the most efficient use of tax dollars and allocation of scarce resources.

A niche strategy also succeeds in serving the public because it allows for the design and development of programs based on real needs of particular subpopulations rather than the development of programs for everyone, including those not interested. Finally, a niche strategy increases the chance of a government or social program's success because the program fits the motivations of those participating in it.

TYPES OF SEGMENTATION

Demographics, behaviors, geographics

In dealing with markets in general and the mature market specifically, the most frequently used way to subdivide markets is demographic characteristics, such as age, sex, income, and education. Researchers measure usage patterns and then compare them across demographic categories.

Another common way to look at submarkets includes examining behaviors such as heavy, light, and nonusage of particular products and users of one brand versus another. Geographic differentiation is still another way to carve up all types of markets, including the mature market.

Measuring what drives purchase

However, dividing or segmenting the market by demographics, geographics, or behavioral measures fails to provide marketing insights in two very significant ways. In the first place, understanding *why* segments differ in consumption is the most important information a marketer can possess and is critical to effective product development and positioning. Knowing only that one region or another, one sex or the other, one age group or another differs in consumption is not enough.

Secondly, demographic and behavioral methods of segmenting explain how people behave with respect to current products in the market. If consumers are faced with several alternatives, none of which meet all of their requirements, they will still choose one. If an alternative enters the marketplace that better meets their needs, the product chosen earlier will lose to the new entry. What consumers have done in the past does not necessarily predict how they will act in the future.

Forecasting the future

As an example, in 1979 in a speech to the Automotive Market Research Council, we pointed out a new consumer segment to the automotive industry. Because of changing technologies, such as electronic ignition, pollution control devices, and the downsizing of cars, a segment of do-it-yourselfers, used to simpler, less-demanding cars, was frustrated. We suggested that those auto repair centers which responded to this opportunity would prosper; those who did not would face problems.

The changes we predicted occurred in the 1980s. Many auto parts stores successfully changed the way they did business, incorporating service bays and consulting kiosks into their operations. These operations were successful because they met the needs of the frustrated do-it-yourselfers. The point is that we were able to see these strategic implications to the automotive aftermarket early, not by examining demographics or behaviors but by examining consumers' frustrations.

WHAT MOTIVATES MATURE CONSUMERS?

A unique approach

Our explanation of the mature market, unlike all others, is based on why older consumers behave as they do. Our three segmentations assess their feelings on being over 50 and finances, feelings about health, and attitudes toward the consumption of food.

Our 50+ description of the forces that underlie and propel the mature market is unique. In Chapter 2, we review numerous studies that assessed this market primarily from a demographic viewpoint. The researchers doing these studies assume that life stage, such as being over or under 65, for example, explains why some seniors behave differently than others. In the chapters that follow, we will show how demographic splits are insufficient to provide marketers with the insights they need to develop effective strategies for the mature market.

Using the most sophisticated research technology available, we have simplified this complex market. By linking attitudes with behaviors and demographics, our 50+ study forms a mosaic for understanding those over 50.

Based on motivational research

Motivational research, derived from clinical psychology, forms the basis of this book. The individual's own thought processes are the variables used to describe his or her actions, rather than demographic or behavioral measures.

Decades ago, motivational researchers believed that purchase decisions were based primarily on unconscious, deep-rooted emotional reasons. One of these earlier motivational researchers, Pierre Martineau, states that the consumer "wants more from life than bargains. And his behavior stems more often from emotional and non-rational causes than from logic."

We regard this view as extreme, and we reject it. Certainly, some of the goods and services people buy are related to self-enhancement. One's choice of beer, perfume, or an automobile may be made on the basis of hopes, fantasies, and dreams, rather than particular functional product characteristics. However, many product decisions are heavily, if not entirely, made on the basis of logical decision-making.

Understanding various appeals

In developing successful strategies for the mature market, both rational and emotional appeals must be understood and exploited. Growing old is a physical as well as an emotional condition. Some women, for example, will buy face cream because the product softens their skin or reduces roughness. These are entirely rational decisions based on the product's ability to perform some function.

Other women, however, will buy face cream because they want to look younger. Understanding what motivates different types of women will lead to more effective appeals, whether they are purely functional, emotional, or a combination of the two.

Our three segmentations of the mature market are based on our assessment of the concerns, motivations, and views of people over 50 about living their lives as they continue to grow older. Their concerns and views about aging are incorporated into both rational and emotional motives for buying products.

OUR RESEARCH PROCESS

Our view of the mature market is based on large and extensive original studies which include purchase information, media usage, activities, health information, demographics, brand images, as well as examinations of attitudinal concerns and views. By collecting an extensive database of information, we are able to link many relationships to form a cohesive picture of the mature market.

Procedure adapted from psychology

To determine the motivational segments that comprise the mature market, we used a procedure from mathematical psychology. The process involves devising a group of attitude statements that reflect the issues to be studied. Three separate groups of statements were used, each concentrating on various aspects of aging and product purchase.

The statements were chosen after reviewing hundreds of articles and numerous books and conversing with professionals involved in providing goods and services to the mature market. For example, the first group of 60 statements focused on growing old and issues about finances:

"I am willing to trust certain financial planners to advise me or make investments for me."

"I am interested in products that will make my skin look younger."

These statements reflect seniors' concerns and views about themselves as older people and were used to determine the Self segments. In two additional sorts, two separate sets of 50 statements each were used to create the Food and Health segmentations.

The statements were sorted by the respondents to indicate their degree of agreement or disagreement. A computer analysis determined groups of people with similar rankings. The motivational segments' needs were understood by examining their rankings of these attitudes.

Reaching attitudinal segments

We then examined purchase and media usage behavior, demographics, and other measures to develop a comprehensive understanding of seniors as consumers. Finally, the entire database was balanced by age, income, census region, and gender to accurately reflect the U.S. population over 50 years of age.

This database forms a basis for the development of general marketing and advertising strategies, expert systems for prospecting and qualifying, and marketing operation models such as quality tracking and product development.

By having such a comprehensive amount of information, to which we continue to add both new data and new respondents, we can determine critical relationships between potential users of products and characteristics that describe them. Knowing, for example, that a segment of seniors pays for financial planning, we can build models to be used in selecting mailing lists. Thus, stockbrokers, insurance agents, and financial planners can achieve greater selling success with more targeted prospecting and direct mail solicitations.

CONCLUSION

This book presents a view of older Americans that makes sense out of their diversity. It gives marketers, government planners, and social service providers greater insights so that they can accomplish their goals using more targeted and efficient strategies.

We examine the market of Americans over the age of 50 from three different perspectives. The first perspective is how they view themselves as older people, especially with regard to their financial situation, mobility, vulnerability to crime, concern about government, retirement, travel, and shopping.

The second view of the mature market looks at them as health consumers. On one hand, this perspective assesses opportunities for marketers of healthcare and pharmaceuticals and, on the other hand, presents a valuable view to social service providers and government healthcare planners.

The third view considers those over 50 as food consumers. Here we describe them as targets for the grocery and packaged goods marketers and for restaurants.

Each of these three views of mature consumers is supported by the attitudes that differentiate them. We connect their attitudes to significant differences in their demographic and behavioral descriptions to provide an understanding of those over 50 as consumers of private, as well as public, products and services. For each view we suggest opportunities and market strategies that will satisfy their needs. This knowledge will provide profitable directions for business and greater efficiencies for public-policy providers.

REFERENCES

Levitt, Theodore, *The Marketing Imagination,* New York: The Free Press, 1983, p. 9.

Levy, Doran J., "The Mind of the Automotive Consumer: Motivations in the Aftermarket," address to the Automotive Market Research Council, October 1979.

Martineau, Pierre, *Motivation in Advertising,* New York: McGraw-Hill, 1957, p. 201.

TWO

WAYS OF SEGMENTING THE MARKET

The appearance of a large gray cloud looming on the demographic horizon was first noted in the professional literature in the late 1950s. The cloud: the immense and ever-increasing mature market.

In 1958, Robert D. Dodge predicted in the *Journal of Retailing* that the mature market would become an important one. "The numbers in this age group," stated Dodge, "will continue to increase, and problems will lessen if marketers understand the nature and characteristics of the market."

Since Dodge's article appeared, over 100 journal articles have addressed ways of thinking about and reaching the mature market. Through 1970 these articles generally stressed the size and importance of the mature population as a whole.

After 1970, researchers began to explore the market's more specific aspects. Many of these later articles focused on different ways of categorizing subgroups of seniors.

ATTEMPTS TO CATEGORIZE MATURE CONSUMERS

A heterogeneous group

The work of marketing researchers was also influenced by gerontologists who believed that seniors were not a homogeneous group, but differed in their adaption to such events as retirement and aging.

As Carol Travis, a social psychologist, points out, children pass through biologi-cally determined "stages." One learns to crawl, for example, before walking. Mature adults, on the other hand, have been more influenced by their environment.

As various industries began to direct their efforts to seniors, their diversity was recognized as problematic. Marketers began to see that a mass-market strategy, which might be effective with other populations, wouldn't work with this group.

During the past 20 years market researchers have placed seniors into categories based on one premise or another. These segmentations or categorizations have been

11

based on a variety of assumptions as to which attributes showed important differences among groups of seniors.

Marketers have recognized that, as developmental psychologist Leonard Pearlin once remarked, "There is not one process of aging, but many; there is not one life course, but many courses; there is no one sequence of stages, but many."

Four common segmentation strategies

In reviewing the segmentation strategies that have been applied to date, we find four types appear repeatedly. These are segmentations based on demographics characteristics, such as age; retirement; psychographics; and lifestyle.

There appears to be some confusion about the meaning of the last two types of segmentation, psychographics and lifestyle. Some writers and researchers use the two words as if they mean the same. For us the word *psychographics* covers a person's hopes, needs, fears, beliefs, opinions, and attitudes which shape how one acts and the choices one makes. We define *lifestyle* as a tangible, external expression of a person's psychographics.

Paula Fitzgerald Bone, an assistant professor of marketing at West Virginia University, found 33 publicly available segmentation studies. Of these segmentations, 16, or 48 percent, are based totally or partially on demographics.

In reviewing the types of segmentation studies completed over the years, there doesn't appear to be any progression from a less sophisticated approach to one that is more comprehensive or complex. Nor has one segmentation strategy dominated the thinking of market researchers over any one period of time.

Segmentation by age appears in 1980, but also crops up in 1989. Although psychographics was first used on the senior market in 1973, it was not used again in publicly available data until 1987. This sporadic use of different types of segmentation strategies suggests that, until now, a definitive or wholly satisfactory way of segmenting seniors had not been developed.

While almost all researchers agree on two points—that seniors are not a homogeneous group and need to be segmented and that seniors are an important market—how to carve up the senior market has received relatively little attention.

Few articles on segmentation of the mature market have actually appeared over the past twenty years in research journals. The bibliographies of these articles show repeated citations to the same studies, many of which were published in the late 1970s.

DEMOGRAPHIC SEGMENTATION

Age-based

The first segmentation strategies based on age appeared almost 15 years ago, and they are continually being put forth. All the authors of these studies have had to face the problem of defining when one becomes a senior. Are we "seniors" at 50 or at 65?

Several researchers have used four age-related segments: 55-64, 65-74, 75-84, and 85 and over. Other researchers have begun their age-based segmentations at 60 or 65.

A second problem for marketers and researchers occurs in considering a person's actual, chronological age versus his or her felt or perceived age. If I am 72 but feel 52, how would you design products for me or create advertisements to capture my attention using an age-based segmentation?

Although age-based segmentations are being used extensively, many researchers question their usefulness. One example is a study, an immense one, commissioned by The Markle Foundation in 1988 to study the "values, attitudes, behavior and overall outlook on life" of America's mature population. The study interviewed 3,000 Americans in person and then segmented respondents according to their age.

One "critical finding" of the Markle study was that ". . . those over 60 tend to be a relatively content and secure group. . . ."

The weakness of categorizing seniors based on one gross variable, such as age, is seen in this statement. Considering that women over 65 comprise 58 percent of those in this age group but 74 percent of the elderly poor, this generalization is misleading. That is, the lives of many elderly women may very well lack "contentment" and "security." Placing all "those over 60" into one general category distorts reality. Some seniors are very content and secure in their lives and others are far less so.

Another example is seen in the study's conclusion that new technologies have not been adopted by seniors because, according to Lloyd N. Morrisett, president of The Markle Foundation, "designed for the convenience and time saving sought by younger people, those technologies simply do not play as large a role in older people's lives." Reporting "averages" within age-based categories, the Markle study could not discern that, in fact, there is a large mature market segment—defined by attitudes and not age—that is highly receptive to new technologies.

In our 50+ study we found that while only 29 percent of the total sample was interested in using a phone to bank or pay bills, 35 percent of the Financial Positives were. The Financial Positives repeatedly show themselves to be far more interested in high-tech devices than the average respondent.

From our perspective, age-based segmentation is a simplistic way of carving up this market. Our position is echoed by Charles D. Schewe, a professor at the University of Massachusetts at Amherst, who comments in the June 1990 issue of *American Demographics* that "The most common segmentation scheme, dividing the market by age, is also generally the most ineffective. Savvy marketers will bypass direct references to age and zero in on the concerns and issues that influence buying."

Financial status

Another demographic approach is to categorize the mature market on its financial status. Considerations based on household income, disposable income, and assets are used to place seniors into categories.

In her article in the January-February 1980 issue of *The Harvard Business Review,* Rena Bartos outlines a segmentation approach that is based on both age and finances. Bartos states that ". . . age by itself is not differentiating enough to reveal the marketing opportunities that exist within it [mature market]." Her belief is that "The socioeconomic conditions that shape people's lives are far more differentiating than age alone."

After outlining six segments, Bartos states that marketers of "general products" need not concern themselves with three of the segments: the poor, the sick, and a segment labeled "other." The remaining three segments are based on age and financial position. These segments, according to Bartos, are the Active Affluents, the Active Retireds, and the Homemakers.

Although the segmentation that Bartos presents provides an interesting perspective, we believe it has certain limitations.

As Bartos herself acknowledges, her segments are not based on an objective, comprehensive, quantifiable study. Bartos fashioned her segments by reviewing U.S. Census data and other available studies. Having completed her analysis, she made an intuitive leap to create the segments she believed should exist.

This specific segmentation is not applicable to the marketing of many products and services. For example, the interests of one product group, healthcare, is not addressed by Bartos's segmentation strategy. She puts to one side that group of seniors who are most ill to focus on those she views as being in largely good health.

In addition, having financial resources does not necessarily mean that one feels motivated to or can actually spend these resources on a particular product or service.

We believe that all demographically based segmentations, whether they are based solely on age or combine age with another variable(s), are too general to be effective marketing tools. Because they present gross generalizations, these segmentations distort reality. They won't lead marketers to their very best prospects.

LIFESTYLE SEGMENTATION

An example of a lifestyle segmentation is a study by Sorce, Tyler, and Loomis. The authors conclude that the "Older American market cannot be viewed as one homogeneous market. . . . The few demographic differences among the segments support the importance of using lifestyle variables to segment this large heterogeneous market."

Six segments emerged from the study. Although it presents interesting insights, the study is limited because it was not based on a national random sample. Respondents were all drawn from a limited geographical area: Rochester, New York.

Shopping orientation segmentation

Based on 373 completed questionnaires, a national study by James R. Lumpkin determined what was important to the elderly in the shopping experience.

Lumpkin's study developed three segments based on shopping orientation. Lumpkin concluded that the results of his study "indicate there are subsegments of the elderly consumer who can be identified by unique shopping orientation profiles." While of obvious interest and application to retailers, such a specific segmentation scheme would be of limited value to those in other industries. In addition, the sample is a small one.

RETIREMENT SEGMENTATION

Retirement has been used in attempts to segment the mature market in a usable and understandable fashion. The basis for this segmentation approach springs from the work of gerontologists who, over the past 30 years, have studied adjustment to retirement.

Limitations of segmenting by retirement

One problem with using retirement as the basis for a segmentation is defining retirement itself. When does retirement occur? How would such a scheme be affected by those who take "early" retirement, who take "late" retirement, or those who never retire at all? And what of those who retire and then return to work part-time? How do they fit into the group of retirees?

A segmentation scheme on retirement may be beneficial in targeting better prospects for only a few products and activities such as golf. But other purchases, such as medical care and foods, do not appear to have any direct connection with whether one has retired or not.

Of those who retire, 83 percent are male. The majority of women who are old enough to retire have not worked outside the home and, therefore, cannot retire. Because of this fact, retirement-based segmentation schemes have included only males.

And yet we know that women represent 58 percent of those over 65. In addition, women are thought to make the vast majority of consumer goods purchases.

Women married to retired men should also be viewed as participating in joint decisions on travel and other leisure activities, as well as decisions made on housing and financial services.

PSYCHOGRAPHIC SEGMENTATION

The earliest attempt to segment persons over 65 by psychographics was completed by Jeffrey G. Towle and Claude R. Martin, Jr. in 1975. Although the study used demographic, psychographic, and buyer style measures, the six segments discovered are based on the "self-concept buyer behavior set."

The authors concluded that the study "did find the existence of natural segments of the elderly market . . . defined by buying style characteristics and it did fit psychographic descriptions to those natural segments that are sensible and operational."

Another early attempt to segment the senior market using psychographics appears in Leonard Fela's dissertation completed 15 years ago. By using psychographics, Fela hoped to arrive at a better understanding of the mature market. Having discovered three psychographic segments, Fela concluded that important differences within the senior market existed.

He suggests that a psychographic segmentation approach can be used to develop new products, select media, create advertising, and find new marketing opportunities.

This work clearly supports the idea that the senior market is not homogeneous but composed of several psychographic subsegments.

VALS and VALS 2

SRI International's Values and Lifestyles (VALS), first introduced in 1978, is a commercially available psychographic segmentation system. VALS 2, introduced in 1989, replaced VALS. Although VALS 2 did not focus on segmenting the mature market, specific segments in VALS 2 are made up heavily of seniors. According to SRI, two-thirds of the Strugglers and Believers segments are mature consumers.

While VALS 2 explores why consumers are buying a product, rather than isolates what they are buying, it has other limitations. The self-orientation dimension that is part of the VALS 2 system, and around which the segments are organized, poses three different motivations for buying.

The system is built on the idea that there is a general and static foundation to purchasing behavior that can be applied to all products and services. The "principle oriented" Believers would be driven by the same underlying motivations in purchasing a car or ice cream or luggage. In contrast to VALS or VALS 2, our approach is specific, linking one population or market to a particular product or service.

The weakness in VALS 2 is acknowledged by Ed Flesch, director of the VALS program, in *Maturity Market Perspectives*. Because of its general approach, we question the usefulness of VALS 2 in segmenting seniors or any other population.

Gerontographics: another attempt

George P. Moschis, a professor of marketing at Georgia State University, approaches understanding the mature market through a model that he calls Gerontographics. In devising his segmentation, Moschis used 136 measures that focused on older adults' needs, attitudes, lifestyles, and behaviors. Through a clustering procedure, he reduced a sample of 3,000 people collected over a three-year period to four segments based on these measures. His four segments reflect various attitudes about health, psychological and social connection with society, consumption, and numerous other categories.

The most unusual facet of Moschis's approach is that he determined the number and names of his segments before he analyzed his data. He states that "the number of subgroupings (segments) and their corresponding names are derived or specified on an *a priori* basis, based on our knowledge about human behavior in late life." As a first step, Moschis determined his segments. Then he collected data that was used to categorize people into his pre-existing segments. The inherent weakness in this approach is that it is based on the assumption that everything about the aging process and the psychological makeup of mature persons is already known. It also assumes that what is now known is perfectly accurate in describing the behavior of older adults. A third weakness in this approach is that it rests on Moschis's ability to be an authoritative and unbiased interpreter of that body of gerontological knowledge.

Our approach was quite different. Our first step was to determine the issues that were important and relevant to persons over 50. However, our segments were determined by the way our respondents answered our questions. In other words, unlike Moschis, we had no predetermined model going into our study.

A second major difference between the 50+ segments and those developed by Moschis is that our segmentation strategies are far more focused. Moschis's four segments combine health, social influences, and consumption. He has compressed the complexity of the mature market into four predefined segments.

In contrast, we did three totally different segmentations. Our 50+ study examines the mature market from three perspectives: self and finances, health, and food. By doing so, our strategies give greater definition for marketers in specific industries.

Moschis himself comments that as he was completing the research on which Gerontographics is based, he found that "older consumers in each of the four segments . . . respond differently to various marketing stimuli across different types of products/services (industry groups) . . . suggesting the need for industry-specific gerontographic segmentation and marketing-response models for greater effectiveness."

Besides the 50+ segmentation strategies, we have gone on to complete proprietary studies for clients, which create new segmentations specific to their market and products or services. At times these proprietary segmentation strategies are linked to our 50+ segments.

Moschis's approach is sophisticated. He makes many of the arguments we do about the need for a multidimensional viewpoint on the issues affecting the older market. However, his model determines only four segments, which are insufficient to answer the needs of marketers in diverse industries. In addition, the development of his segments is limited in that it is based on his interpretation of existing gerontological literature. We believe Gerontographics presents a far too restricted view of the mature market.

SEGMENTING BY MEDIA USAGE

A segmentation study using psychographic variables was conducted by Ellen Day, Brian Davis, Rhonda Dove, and Warren French to study whether or not segments exist within the mature market. A second objective was to determine whether or not those segments could be reached effectively through media.

The study found four segments that differed in their consumption of the media. The authors concluded that "media habits vary considerably within the elderly population. Therefore, in order to reduce the amount of waste in trying to reach this group, a segmentation approach to advertising is not only appropriate but virtually imperative."

The authors go on to apply their findings not only to media selection but to the appropriate messages and images that should be used in advertising aimed at one of these segments. How effectively one can apply the results of this study to the mature market as a whole is, however, questionable. The data is based on a sample of 111 married females over 65. The sample itself is so small that projections on the size of the segments are problematical. There are also other limitations.

Considering the fact that 58 percent of women over 65 are widowed, single, or divorced, the data cannot be taken to represent the media habits of all women in this age group. And because only women were interviewed, the conclusions obviously do not cover the media habits of men over 65.

CONCLUSION

While the need to segment the senior population has been established, the segmentation approaches that have been used to date to categorize a diverse senior population have been only partially successful.

The result has been some confusion over the actual nature of the senior market. One study states that seniors are extremely brand loyal, another study suggests that they are willing to switch brands. Study "A" concludes that seniors are frightened of high-tech products, whereas study "B" finds them willing to try new innovative products.

It isn't surprising that the results of these studies appear contradictory and confusing. The problem with many of these studies is that samples are often extremely small and often limited to a specific city or locale. The methodologies used in these studies to segment the mature market have frequently produced partial views, rather than comprehensive, targeted scenarios.

At times the basis for a segmentation has been too general, as in the case of an age-based approach, or too narrow, as in the case of retirement-based studies. To capture the complexities of this population, attention must be paid to its many facets. Rather than segment seniors based on only one variable, such as shopping behavior or media usage, what's needed is a comprehensive approach that will take into account an entire range of variables. Psychographics, including motivations and needs; behaviors; demographics; media usage; and lifestyle issues, must all be considered *simultaneously* in order to develop realistic and effective segments within the senior population. Our 50+ segmentation strategies combine all of these elements to allow marketers to both understand and reach their best targets within the mature market.

The growing diversity of the mature market and increasing competition demand that we improve in our ability to target our best prospects. Because of these trends, future segmentations will not only have to be comprehensive in how they segment the market but also specific to a product or service.

We are doing such segmentations on all age groups, not just those over 50, as we regularly develop product-specific strategies for clients. Besides providing more directly relevant insights, these specific segmentation strategies allow our clients to more precisely focus on reaching their best prospects.

REFERENCES

Bartos, Rena, "Over 49: The Invisible Consumer Market," *The Harvard Business Review,* January-February 1980, pp. 140-148.

Bone, Paula Fitzgerald, "Identifying Mature Segments," *Journal of Consumer Marketing,* Fall 1991, pp. 19-32.

Day, Ellen, Brian Davis, Rhonda Dove, and Warren French, "Reaching the Senior Citizen Market(s)," *Journal of Advertising Research,* December 1987-January 1988, pp. 23-30.

Dodge, Robert D., "Selling the Older Consumer," *Journal of Retailing,* Summer 1958, pp. 73-81, 100.

Fela, Leonard John, "The Elderly Consumer Market: A Psychographic Segmentation Study," Ph.D. dissertation, Syracuse University, 1977.

Gelb, Betsy, "Discovering the 65+ Consumer," *Business Horizons,* May-June 1982, pp. 42-46.

Lumpkin, James R., "Shopping Orientation Segmentation of the Elderly Consumer," *Journal of the Academy of Marketing Science,* Spring 1985, pp. 271-289.

Maturity Market Perspectives, December 1989, p. 7. Source of comments by Ed Flesch on VALS2.

Morrisett, Lloyd N., President, The Markle Foundation, letter to Carol Morgan, June 11, 1988.

Moschis, George P., "Gerontographics: A Scientific Approach to Analyzing and Targeting the Mature Market," *Journal of Services Marketing,* Summer 1992, pp. 17-25.

"Pioneers on the Frontier of Life: Aging in America," The Markle Foundation, Executive Summary, 1988, p. 1.

Schewe, Charles D., "Get in Position for the Older Market," *American Demographics,* June 1990, pp. 38-41, 61-63.

Sorce, Patricia, Philip R. Tyler, and Lynette M. Loomis, "Lifestyles of Older Americans," *Journal of Consumer Marketing,* Summer 1989, pp. 53-63.

Towle, Jeffrey G., and Claude R. Martin Jr., "The Elderly Consumer: One Segment or Many?" *Advances in Consumer Research,* 1975, pp. 463-468.

THREE

THE IMPORTANCE OF THE MATURE MARKET

"That's where the money is!"

This was the response of a famous bank robber when asked why he robbed banks. And so it is with America's aging population. Households headed by persons over 50 constitute 43 percent of all American households. Census figures show that the median net worth of households in the 50 to 65 age group is $68,749 and $73,471 for households over 65. These net worth figures are approximately twice that of the median net worth for all U.S. households: $35,752. Wealth is so concentrated in the mature component of the U.S. population that marketers can no longer ignore it.

High discretionary incomes

Besides having amassed a high net worth, households over 50 also have a high level of spendable discretionary income. *A Marketer's Guide to Discretionary Income* defines such income as what is left over after taxes and "expenditures 30 percent greater than the average for households of a similar size, age, and region of residence."

Those over 50 in the U.S. population control 43 percent of all spendable discretionary income. While discretionary income averages $12,332 for all U.S. households that have such income, it rises to $13,285 when only households over 50 are considered.

These figures are misleading, however, because households of those over 50 are smaller than those under 50. By factoring in their smaller household size, per capita discretionary income is actually higher among those over 50 than under 50. For example, at $6,280, per capita discretionary income is highest among households headed by 65- to 69-year-olds.

We see, then, that contrary to the stereotype of cash-strapped mature consumers, those over 50 have, on a per capita basis, more money to spend on nonessential products and services.

21

Pressuring government

In addition to high assets and disposable incomes, the increasing numbers of those over 50 have considerable impact on government. Because the majority of seniors recognize their power as a political voting block, they exert enormous pressure on politicians. In 1989 services to those over 65 consumed 29 percent of the federal budget.

One example of these federal outlays for the mature population is that of long-term nursing home care. In 1990, the United States spent $60 billion on long-term care. Only 2 percent of this amount was covered by long-term care insurance. Two government programs, Medicare and Medicaid, covered 53 percent of such care at a cost of $53 billion.

A diverse population

In this book, we will describe the mature population as both a marketing target and as recipients of social services. Marketers, politicians, and public planners must understand that the over-50 population is very diverse. To achieve one's goal to market a product or create a successful government policy is not an "all or nothing" phenomenon. Groups of seniors will react differently to various products or services depending on how they view their lives, health, and economic situations.

A GROWING MARKET

Between now and the year 2000, the number of 18- to 34-year-olds will shrink by 9 million and lose $40 billion a year in buying power; those over 50 will gain 12 million people and $300 billion a year in buying power.

Through the next two decades, the over-50 population will continue to grow, according to the U.S. Census, by 2 to 3 percent every five years. In 1995, 27 percent of the population will be over 50. That percentage will increase to 29 percent in 2000, 31 percent in 2005, and 34 percent in 2010.

Where is growth coming from?

This growth in older Americans will include men, as well as women. Thomas Exter, writing for *American Demographics,* points out that the number of men in their 60s will increase by at least 75 percent to 17 million; the number of women in this age group will increase at least 68 percent, to 19 million.

Amazingly enough, the fastest growing age cohort is people age 90 to 100, which has increased 42 percent in the last decade. Americans are living longer than any people have ever lived before. The trend toward an even longer lifespan will continue, and the ranks of the very old will swell.

Baby Boomers turn 50

The most significant component of the U.S. population, in terms of percentages, is the Baby Boomers. Likened to the bulge a pig makes as a python digests it, this huge group has produced profound changes in the American society. The Baby Boomers, born in the 20 years following World War II, have greatly affected patterns of education, housing, and consumption.

Because of their sheer numbers, the Baby Boomers and their changing needs have always been a major target for marketers. In only a few years, their needs will change again as the oldest of the Baby Boomers turn 50 in 1996. Marketers who ignore the senior market today will have a difficult time getting a foothold serving the needs of aging Boomers. Planning now is essential.

THE MATURE AS CONSUMERS, EMPLOYEES

Even without the Baby Boomers, the senior market is already huge. Today, much of the revenues generated for many product and service categories comes from people over the age of 50.

Spending their money

Each year, according to the U.S. Travel Data Center, those over 50 take 163 million trips and account for:

- 72 percent of recreational vehicle (RV) trips
- 70 percent of motorcoach excursions
- 70 percent of all cruise passengers
- 44 percent of all adult passport holders
- 34 percent of all purchasers of overseas packaged tours

Americans over 65, who constitute 12 percent of the U.S. population, consume 30 percent of all prescription drugs, according to the *Mature Market Report*. Yankelovich Clancy Shulman points out that those over 50 buy 40 percent of all healthcare products. Today 53 million grandparents buy 25 percent of all toys sold.

Source of labor

The senior market, aside from its importance as a consuming group, is also an important source of labor. Many may find the assertion that the United States is facing a shortage of labor hard to believe, given recent high unemployment statistics. But in the 1990s the population over 50 will grow 19 percent; those under 50, only 4 percent. This means that unless there is a huge influx of young immigrants, much of the country's labor needs will have to be filled by increasingly older workers.

Many companies are recognizing the importance of working seniors. Since 1989, Day's Inn has sponsored a Senior Power Job Fair, bringing together 2,000 companies and 23,000 older job seekers. Fast food companies, such as McDonald's, have recognized the value of older workers on counter crews and are now moving them into supervisory positions. Traveler's Insurance has hired 750 seniors as consultants.

As volunteers, seniors represent a major source of labor. According to the Marriott Corporation, 41 percent of seniors currently volunteer almost four hours a day for 64 days a year, the equivalent of 32 working days. The American Association of Retired

Persons (AARP) claims that 30 percent of those over 55 do some volunteer work. SCORE, the Service Corps of Retired Executives, has over 30,000 volunteer retirees who offer advice and experience to emerging entrepreneurs.

SOME (BAD) REASONS FOR AVOIDING THIS MARKET

How can it be that so many marketers continue to ignore the over-50 market? To obtain support for our 50+ study, we talked to hundreds of marketing executives in many different industries throughout the United States; we were surprised by the responses we got.

Seniors too brand loyal

An executive at a cosmetics company explained that by the time women reached their 50s, they were intensely brand loyal. Since that was the case, it would be a waste of time and money, her company reasoned, to try to convert older women to their brands. Our study shows that for some products and for some of our 50+ segments, her company's assessment is correct. For example, for hair dye or coloring, 82 percent of the female users are loyal to one brand; however, for face cream, the percentage of female single-brand users drops to 63 percent. Brand loyalty can be defined only in the context of particular product categories.

But what about new products? One of the wealthier segments we will introduce you to in this book does not like the idea of getting old or, more particularly, looking old. Therefore, opportunities for the cosmetics industry may lie in the creation of innovative products with totally new promises that address the issues of this segment or other segments.

Unfavorable image associated with seniors

Probably the most typical reason for ignoring the over-50 population is a fear of creating brand imagery that would hurt sales to the under-50 population. "We don't want young people to think our brand is only for old folks." A component of this mindset is that the over 50s are going to die off soon. Consequently, these marketers have decided the best place to invest over the long term is with the younger population.

Automobile executives who hold this view, for example, might be surprised to know that persons over 50, according to Yankelovich Clancy Shulman, buy 43 percent of all new cars. Furthermore, the average age of buyers of American-made luxury cars is 65. In other words, taking the long-term view and concentrating on the younger market ignores the reality of the enormity and wealth of today's senior market.

Difficult to reach

They are too hard to reach! This reason to avoid seniors ignores the sophistication of the direct marketing industry that targets many specific groups—seniors included. Additionally, as the media continue to fragment to attract very select groups, more communication outlets are opening up. Increasingly, these, such as *Nostalgia* and *Longevity*, as well as a raft of senior publications, target mature adults.

Seniors are all the same

Marketing executives also avoid marketing to seniors because they view them too simplistically. Many people still visualize the senior market as made up of poor old ladies with blue hair and creased shopping bags. While it is certainly true that there are many poor women—and men—in this component of the population, this stereotype was more true 30 years ago and is far less accurate today. For example, in 1959, 43 percent of the mature population lived in poverty; by 1987, their numbers had diminished to 12 percent.

NEW WAY OF THINKING

In this book we are advocating a new way to think about marketing. Our new perspectives should, we believe, be applied to all marketing efforts, regardless of age. These views are, however, especially useful for applications to the booming and exceptionally diverse mature market. Our innovative thinking encompasses the following views:

1. *What happened in the past will not necessarily happen in the future.* Business must continue to evolve by adapting to changing conditions. The proactive marketer will constantly examine the marketplace's varying needs to avoid becoming out-of-date. As the Baby Boomers enter the mature market, for example, their lifestyles will be different from those seniors born prior to the end of World War II. This book shows how different types of people think about growing old and how these patterns of thought affect buying behavior.

2. *Knowledge is a form of capital.* Businesses must invest in information. The information needed to operate a successful business is as important as the machinery used to produce its products. Allowing know-how to become stale and outdated is as bad as letting machines rust. This book presents marketers with a major database and shows how the information can be used for efficient, profitable strategies.

3. *Over-simplistic thinking is self-defeating.* Markets are complicated and the tendency to oversimplify is a common pitfall. Not all seniors are alike. Their financial situation, educational achievement, social class, and other factors make them a very diverse market. This book describes three major perspectives that drive their purchase behaviors.

4. *Egocentric marketing is likely to fail.* The marketing manager who relies on his or her own intuition about how consumers buy is walking on thin ice. Managers must recognize and understand consumers who are not like them in order to create successful products and services for the mature marketplace.

5. *Long-term thinking is crucial for long-term survival.* The mature market is already a major market. As the huge Baby Boom component merges with older seniors into the mature market, however, opportunities will explode. The time for planning one's strategy is now, before old or new competitors preempt your possibilities.

6. *Segmented or target marketing is ultimately more successful than mass marketing.* Mass marketers try to simplify their production and marketing by appealing to

the largest number of consumers. This lowest common denominator approach makes mass marketers vulnerable to specialty marketers who appeal to special interest segments. In this book, we will carve up the mature market so that you can select particular segments as targets. With specific mature consumers' needs in mind, you will be able to focus your design, production, and promotion efforts.

CONCLUSION

The point of our research and this book is that the population over 50 is very diverse and possesses a great amount of America's wealth. Various groups in this population, differentiated by needs, purchase patterns, and lifestyles, represent huge opportunities for marketers.

In the following chapters, we will introduce you to different types of seniors and point out opportunities in numerous industries. By understanding how these different segments relate to products and services, you will have a foundation for developing profitable ventures for this very important market.

REFERENCES

Exter, Thomas, "How Big Will the Older Market Be?" *American Demographics*, June 1990, pp. 30-36.

"Fast Facts," *Mature Market Report*, May 1992, p.7.

"Household Net Worth—Percent Distribution, by Selected Characteristics: 1988," *Statistical Abstract of the United States,* 1991, Table 760, p. 469.

Maren, Michael, "Catch the Age Wave," *Success,* October 1991, pp. 54-56.

"Projections of the Total Population by Age, Sex, and Race: 1995-2010," *Statistical Abstract of the United States,* 1991, Table 18, p. 16.

"Spotlight: The 50-Plus Market," *Adweek's Marketing Week,* July 22, 1991. Source of citations from Yankelovich Clancy Shulman.

Townsend, Bickley, "Fun Money," *American Demographics,* October 1989, pp. 39-41. Source of citation from *A Marketer's Guide to Discretionary Income.*

PART TWO

THE SELF SEGMENTS: ATTITUDES TOWARD LIFE, AGING, AND FINANCES

FOUR

THE FOUR SELF SEGMENTS

The immense financial clout wielded by those over 50 in the United States should be taken into account by every sector. From dollars invested in the stock market to refurbishing empty nests, mature Americans are spending. They have a median net worth that is twice that of the average U.S. population and control 43 percent of all spendable discretionary income. How people feel about themselves and their financial situation very much influences their willingness to buy. Because of this, our study of the 50+ market included a segmentation on self-perception and finances.

In completing our segmentation process, respondents sorted 60 statements into piles according to their levels of agreement or disagreement. These statements included the following:

- I wish I could move to a safer neighborhood.
- Plastic surgery is something I would consider to keep looking younger.
- I believe the best years of my life are now and in the future.
- I feel really secure about my financial future.
- I believe it is important for an older person to know how to use a gun.
- I like the idea of a working retirement where I can work if I want, when I want, and for whom I want.

Four segments developed from the segmentation methodology we've described in Chapter 1. These segments are the Upbeat Enjoyers, the Insecure, the Threatened Actives, and the Financial Positives.

THE UPBEAT ENJOYER SEGMENT

The Upbeat Enjoyers, 22 percent of the over-50 population, are enthusiastic, active, and involved (see Figure 4–1). They believe they are successful and are optimistic about their futures.

**Figure 4–1   Segment Size,
50+ Self Segments**

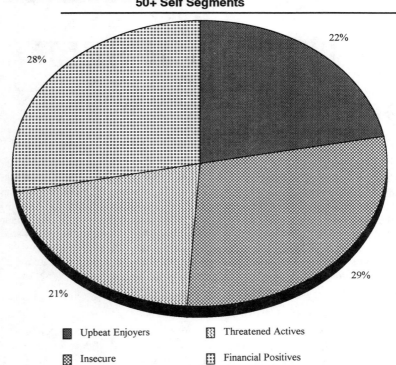

The four Self segments include the Upbeat Enjoyers (22 percent), Insecure (29 percent), Threatened Actives (21 percent), and Financial Positives (28 percent).

Happy past, bright future

Far more than the other segments, the Upbeat Enjoyers feel that their best years are now and those yet to come. They have a positive attitude toward life and are the segment most likely to agree that their quality of life is linked to an openness to change.

The Upbeat Enjoyers believe they are successful people who have been lucky in life. They, along with the Financial Positives, are the segment least likely to report frequent feelings of loneliness.

Little concern with finances

When asked about their finances, the Upbeat Enjoyers really don't have much to say. They do not appear to be particularly concerned about investments, savings, or future financial security.

When asked to prioritize several issues, including finances, the Upbeat Enjoyers gave other interests and topics higher priority. While all the other segments feel that "being financially secure" is a major concern, the Upbeat Enjoyers do not.

Looking and feeling great

Upbeat Enjoyers are significantly different from the other segments in their attitude toward their appearance. When compared to the other segments, only the Upbeat Enjoyers agree that they have become more attractive with age, and that they are "sexier than ever."

The Upbeat Enjoyers are the only segment that is really satisfied with their appearance, even though they believe they live in a society "too focused on youth and beauty." Those in this segment would not consider plastic surgery to keep themselves looking younger.

As the only segment that believes that "gray hair looks great," the Upbeat Enjoyers are not interested in products that would return gray hair to its original color.

Although they would not change their appearance through the use of surgery or cosmetics, the Upbeat Enjoyers clearly want to look attractive. In relation to clothing, only the Upbeat Enjoyers say that wearing the latest styles makes them feel good.

Not only do the Upbeat Enjoyers believe they look good, but they feel good too. They are the only segment to agree that they feel much younger than they are. In fact, this is a perception with which the Upbeat Enjoyers very strongly agree.

Staying active important to them

This segment, much more than any other, wants to enjoy life and remain active—both mentally and physically. For example, the Upbeat Enjoyers are the only segment interested in going on cruises. Enjoying life for this segment means sitting on a beach—their idea of a great vacation.

The Upbeat Enjoyers also favor taking long trips by car or recreational vehicle (RV) and feel comfortable about making their own arrangements without depending on a travel agent.

The Upbeat Enjoyers don't limit themselves to fun and games when it comes to activities. They are also interested in more intellectual pursuits. The Upbeat Enjoyers are the only Self segment to express an interest in going to lectures and taking courses through the mail or on television. They also enjoy day trips to educational attractions, such as museums.

The Upbeat Enjoyers clearly feel capable of continued intellectual pursuits, as they are the only segment that does not believe that their memories are worsening with age.

Because they don't feel totally dependent on their cars, it follows that the Upbeat Enjoyers do not oppose laws requiring the retesting of older people for driver's licenses.

A "working retirement"

Upbeat Enjoyers do, however, have very strong feelings about how they want to spend their retirement. In keeping with their active lifestyle, they are likely to report that they don't believe in retirement at all but always want to "work at something."

The Upbeat Enjoyers also agree very strongly that they will enjoy retirement as long as they can work when and where they want. The fact that the Upbeat Enjoyers are the only segment interested in doing more volunteer work "in the coming years" signals their willingness to consider unpaid, as well as paid, work after retirement.

Minimal safety concerns

The Upbeat Enjoyers, who are trying to live life to its fullest, aren't preoccupied with safety concerns. The only segment that does not feel increasingly concerned about being crime victims, the Upbeat Enjoyers are strongly against the idea of older people learning how to use guns. Those in this segment don't wish to move to a safer neighborhood.

Find condominiums appealing

While all other Self segments agree that they would like to "spend the rest of their lives in their own homes," the Upbeat Enjoyers feel less strongly about this idea. In fact, the idea of living in a condominium is appealing to the Upbeat Enjoyers, the only segment enthusiastic about this idea. When the Upbeat Enjoyers "need help in deciding on where to live," they won't rely on their children.

Open to mail order

The Upbeat Enjoyers are concerned about looking good. With their busy and active lifestyles, however, it's not surprising that they turn to catalogs for their purchases. They are, in fact, the only Self segment that feels positive about using mail order.

Although they claim that value is a major concern when making a purchase, the Upbeat Enjoyers aren't looking for senior discounts. They don't find it difficult to get around in stores while shopping and are the only segment that isn't interested in stores having chairs on which to rest.

DEMOGRAPHICS—THE UPBEAT ENJOYERS

Females the majority

In comparison to the total U.S. population over 50 (58 percent), fewer of the Upbeat Enjoyers are females (56 percent) (see Figure 4–2). Although the Upbeat Enjoyers are predominantly female, this segment is not the most dominated by females. There are far more female Insecure (65 percent) than female Upbeat Enjoyers.

Youngest Self segment

The youngest of the four Self segments, the Upbeat Enjoyers have a median age of 62 years. Compared to only 18 percent of all those over 50, more Upbeat Enjoyers (23 percent) are between the ages of 50 and 55 (see Figure 4–3).

Most divorced, least widowed

As opposed to 7 percent of the over-50 population, 10 percent of the Upbeat Enjoyers are divorced or separated, making them the most divorced or separated of the Self segments. However, more of the Upbeat Enjoyers (63 percent) are also married, in comparison to all those over 50 (58 percent).

Only one in five of the Upbeat Enjoyers are widowed, compared to 44 percent of the Insecure and 30 percent of the U.S. population over 50 (see Figure 4–4).

Figure 4–2   Gender, 50+ Self Segments

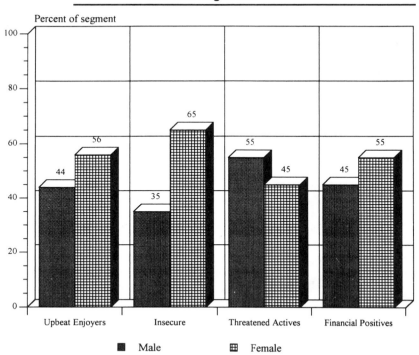

Of the four segments, only the Threatened Actives segment has more males than females. Compared to the other three segments, more of the Insecure are female.

Among most highly educated

Upbeat Enjoyers are one of the two Self segments with the highest level of education, a median of 13 years. Far more of this sample (32 percent) has four years of college or more as compared to the over-50 population (26 percent) and the Insecure and Threatened Actives (22 percent each) (see Figure 4–5). In fact, far more of the Upbeat Enjoyers (23 percent) as compared to all those over 50 (17 percent) completed at least some postgraduate work.

Financially secure

With a median income of $37,112, the Upbeat Enjoyers have the second highest income level of the four Self segments. A third of the Upbeat Enjoyers have annual before-tax household incomes of $50,000 or more, compared to only a quarter of the U.S. population over 50. In contrast to the Upbeat Enjoyers, only 10 percent of the Insecure have incomes in this range (see Figure 4–6).

The Upbeat Enjoyers also have the second highest level of assets, excluding their homes, of the four Self segments, a median of $70,617. This level of assets is far higher than that of the U.S. population over 50 ($43,743).

Living in the Northeast

Slightly more than half of the Upbeat Enjoyers live in the Northeast (28 percent) and Midwest (25 percent) census regions. While 35 percent of the total U.S. population over 50 is from the South, only 27 percent of the Upbeat Enjoyers live in this region, fewer than any other segment (see Figure 4–7).

Work, work, work

More of the Upbeat Enjoyers than of the other three Self segments work for pay each week. Seventy-five percent, as compared to only 59 percent of the over-50 population, work either full time or part time (see Figure 4–8).

Professionals, technicals, managers

When it comes to the Upbeat Enjoyers' careers, almost half are now in or were in white collar positions. More of the Upbeat Enjoyers than any other segment have spent their lives working in professional or technical positions (33 percent). In addition, 16 percent worked as managers or executives, 13 percent as clerical workers, and 8 percent as homemakers.

Postponing retirement

The Upbeat Enjoyers are the least likely of all the Self segments to have retired. In comparison to 51 percent of the total U.S. population over 50, only 39 percent of the Upbeat Enjoyers have retired with no intention of returning to work. In contrast, 63 percent of the Financial Positives have done so (see Figure 4–9).

**Figure 4–3   Age,
50+ Self Segments**

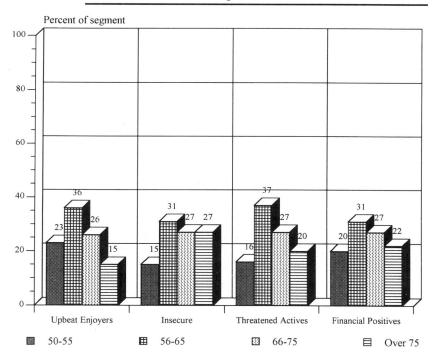

More Upbeat Enjoyers, compared to the other segments, are between the ages of 50 and 55.
In contrast, more Insecure are in the over-75 category.

More returning to work

More of the Upbeat Enjoyers who have retired have returned to work. Forty-one
percent of those in this segment who have retired have been employed either part time
or full time since retirement as compared to only 29 percent of the over-50 population
(see Figure 4–9).

Business owners after retirement

Of those Upbeat Enjoyers who have returned to work after retirement, 9 percent
became business owners or entrepreneurs, compared to only 6 percent of all those over
50. In addition, 26 percent took professional or technical positions compared to only
15 percent of the over-50 population. On the other hand, while 24 percent of the U.S.
population over 50 became homemakers after retirement, only 18 percent of the
Upbeat Enjoyers did so.

**Figure 4–4   Marital Status,
50+ Self Segments**

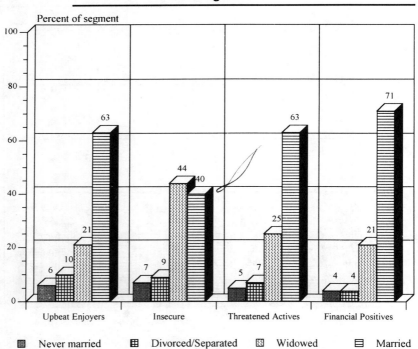

More of the Financial Positives, compared to the other segments, are married, while more of the Insecure are widowed.

Doing the most volunteer work

Fifty-seven percent of those in this segment do some volunteer work, far more than the over-50 population (45 percent) and significantly more than the Insecure (32 percent) and Threatened Actives (39 percent).

Demographic summary

The Upbeat Enjoyers are the youngest, the most divorced, and the least widowed of the four Self segments. One of the most highly educated of the Self segments, the Upbeat Enjoyers have both the second highest median annual income and the second highest level of assets of these segments. More of the Upbeat Enjoyers live in the Northeast than in any other region.

The least likely to retire from the professional or technical and managerial positions they now hold, more of the Upbeat Enjoyers work for pay and volunteer their time. In addition, they are the most likely to return to work after retirement, becoming business owners or taking professional or technical positions.

THE INSECURE SEGMENT

The second segment, the Insecure, are 29 percent of the over-50 population (see Figure 4–1). The Insecure are very troubled about their financial well-being. They are also the most pessimistic about their appearance and their futures.

Pessimistic about past and future

Far more than the other segments, the Insecure feel the best years of their lives are over. In addition, only the Insecure feel that they have been unlucky in life and haven't been successful.

The Insecure face an unhappy future with memories of a grim past. And these memories are fading as the Insecure report that their memories aren't as good as they used to be. Clearly, when compared to the other three Self segments, those in the Insecure segment are the most pessimistic about their future. Only the isolated Insecure report often feeling lonely. However, they are the only Self segment that envisions reaching out for someone to help them plan, should they become very ill.

Resistant to change

Although the Insecure believe being open to change is important to their quality of life, they appear resistant to it. For example, the Insecure would be happiest if they could live out their lives in their own homes.

The Insecure also don't like the way American values are changing. They do, however, very strongly agree that terminally ill people should have the right to stop their own treatment.

Uncertain about financial security

Not having enough money to live on is the one issue that sets the Insecure apart from the other three segments. It comes as no surprise that the Insecure agree with the statement "I have to admit most of my investments are conservative."

Those in this segment strongly agree that being financially secure is a major concern. This is the statement with which the Insecure have the highest level of agreement—far higher than that of the Threatened Actives and the Financial Positives, who are also concerned with financial security.

The Insecure are the only segment that feel uncertain about their financial future. Worried about their finances, Insecures want a retirement where they can work if, when, and for whom they want.

Little to pass on

On one hand, the Insecure, who have so little, are the only segment to claim that their resources will be spent on their needs. Their children can "fend for themselves."

However, they also deny that they will rely on their children when they can no longer care for themselves.

Uncomfortable with appearance

The process of aging for the Insecure is a negative one. Living in a society they find too focused on youth and beauty, they believe that they themselves have become less attractive with age and don't feel "sexier than ever." Feeling it is important to look as young as possible, the Insecure are interested in products that will make their skin look younger. They are the only segment interested in using products that return gray hair to its original color.

Day trips and discounts

Although the Insecure agree somewhat that they are "totally dependent" on their cars to get around, they are not opposed to the legislature passing a law requiring special retesting of older people for driver's licenses.

The Insecure segment are not planning for a particularly active retirement. However, they do enjoy going on escorted tours and day trips to attractions such as museums. When traveling, the Insecure are the segment most interested in receiving special discounts for people over the age of 50 from hotels and airlines.

Concerned about crime

Although more concerned than ever about being crime victims, the Insecure don't believe older people need to learn how to use guns.

Shop for value

The Insecure prefer to shop in well-established stores they know and are likely to shop for value. Although they don't expect special courtesy from salespeople due to their age, they would like stores to provide shoppers with more chairs for resting.

DEMOGRAPHICS—THE INSECURE

Predominantly females

Compared to only 58 percent of the over-50 population, 65 percent of the Insecure are females. This segment contains far more females than any other Self segment, especially in contrast to the Threatened Actives, only 45 percent of whom are females (see Figure 4–2).

Oldest Self segment

The oldest of the four Self segments, the Insecure have a median age of 66 years. Twenty-seven percent of the Insecure are over 75 as compared to 23 percent of all those over 50 and only 15 percent of the Upbeat Enjoyers (see Figure 4–3).

**Figure 4–5   Level of Education,
50+ Self Segments**

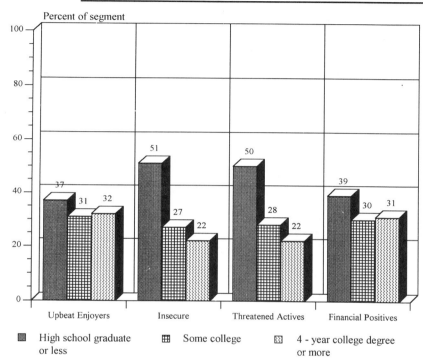

Highly educated, nearly one-third of both the Upbeat Enjoyers and Financial Positives have one college degree or more.

Widows and widowers

The Insecure are the most widowed and the least married of the Self segments. Whether because of widowhood, divorce, or never having married, more than half (60 percent) of the Insecure are not married.

Far more Insecure (44 percent) are widowed as compared to the U.S. population over 50 (30 percent). The contrast is even more dramatic when the percentage of those widowed among the Insecure is compared to those among the Financial Positives and the Upbeat Enjoyers (21 percent each). In addition, 9 percent of the Insecure are divorced or separated and 7 percent never married (see Figure 4–4).

Lacking a strong education

With a median of 11 years of education, the Insecure, along with the Threatened Actives, are among the least educated of the four Self segments. Fifty-one percent of the Insecure are high school graduates or less as compared to 45 percent of the U.S. population over 50.

In addition, compared to 26 percent of the national mature population, only 22 percent of the Insecure have four years of college or more. Almost a third of the Financial Positives and Upbeat Enjoyers have one college degree or more (see Figure 4–5).

Poorest Self segment

The Insecure have by far the lowest annual before-tax household income of the Self segments: a median of $11,001. While a quarter of the U.S. population over 50 has an income of $50,000 or more, only 10 percent of the Insecure do. In contrast, one-third of the Financial Positives and Upbeat Enjoyers enjoy incomes in this range.

In fact, compared to 30 percent of the over-50 population, almost half (49 percent) of the Insecure have annual before-tax incomes of less than $10,000 (see Figure 4–6).

Figure 4–6   Annual Pre-Tax Household Income, 50+ Self Segments

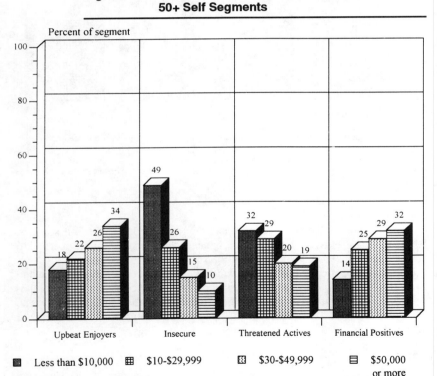

Approximately one-third of the Upbeat Enjoyers and Financial Positives have annual pre-tax household incomes of $50,000 or more. In contrast, nearly half of the Insecure have incomes of less than $10,000.

The Insecure also have the fewest assets of the Self segments. They have a median of $24,130 in assets, not counting their homes, far less than the over-50 population ($43,743) and in sharp contrast to the Financial Positives ($97,074).

Southerners, Midwesterners

More Insecure live in the South census region (32 percent) than in any other. In addition, more of the Insecure (30 percent) than of any other segment live in the Midwest. Twenty-four percent of those in this segment reside in the Northeast. On the other hand, while 18 percent of the U.S. population over 50 lives in the West, only 14 percent of the Insecure do so (see Figure 4–7).

Fewer working

The Insecure are the least likely of the Self segments to work for pay. Fewer Insecure work either part time or full time (48 percent) as compared to the national population over 50 (59 percent). In contrast, three-quarters of the Upbeat Enjoyers do such work (see Figure 4–8).

More clerical workers and homemakers

Sixteen percent of the Insecure report having spent their working lives employed as clerical workers. Another 16 percent were homemakers, compared to 10 percent of the over-50 population. In addition, significantly more Insecure than all those over 50 worked as salespeople (9 percent), laborers (8 percent), service workers (7 percent), and farmers (3 percent).

Although 17 percent of the Insecure currently hold professional or technical positions or held them before retirement, 24 percent of the over-50 population do so. In contrast, 33 percent of the Upbeat Enjoyers hold or have held such jobs.

Retiring at average rate

Retiring from a job with no intention of returning to work has been done by half of the Insecure, virtually the same as the over-50 population (see Figure 4–9).

More returning to work

Far more of the Insecure (36 percent) have been employed either full time or part time since retirement, as compared to all those over 50 (29 percent) (see Figure 4–9).

Homemakers, clericals after retirement

Of those Insecure who returned to work after retirement, 32 percent became homemakers, far more than any other segment. In addition, compared to one out of eight of the U.S. population over 50, one out of five of the Insecure became clerical workers after retirement.

Volunteering less

While a third of the Insecure volunteer, far more of the U.S. population over 50 (45 percent) and Upbeat Enjoyers (57 percent) do so.

Demographic summary

Containing far more females, the Insecure segment is the oldest and most widowed of the four Self segments. They, along with the Threatened Actives, are the least educated and have the lowest median annual household income and level of assets of these segments. More of the Insecure live in the South than in any other region. In addition, more Insecure are Midwesterners.

While half of those in this segment have retired, far more of the Insecure who have retired have returned to work—most to clerical and homemaking positions. The Insecure, however, are the least likely of the Self segments to work full time or to volunteer.

THE THREATENED ACTIVE SEGMENT

The Threatened Actives, the third Self segment, comprise 21 percent of the population over 50 (see Figure 4–1). Those in this segment want to continue working, remain in their own homes, and keep driving their cars.

Optimistic outlook on life

Although very concerned about their own safety, the Threatened Actives still have a generally positive outlook on life. Despite their fears, the Threatened Actives feel they have been successful, and believe that the best years of their lives are now and in the future. The Threatened Actives don't believe their memories are as good as they used to be, however.

Resistant to change

The Threatened Actives appear resistant to change. In terms of housing, they would like to continue living in their own homes for the rest of their lives. Even though they are getting older, the Threatened Actives want to continue doing those things that are important to them, such as drive their cars. Paralleling these views is this segment's disagreement with the idea that openness to change is important to the quality of their lives.

Along with the Insecure, the Threatened Actives aren't comfortable with the way American values are changing. They do agree, although at a low level, that terminally ill patients should have the right to discontinue medical treatment at any time they desire.

Financially independent

The Threatened Actives feel somewhat that their financial security is a major concern, as it is for three of the four segments. However, they do agree at a low level that they are secure about their financial future. An independent group, the Threatened Actives are the only segment opposed to listening to financial planners for advice.

Will provide for children

Only the Threatened Actives are willing to spend some of their savings on their children, rather than solely on themselves.

Appearance not important

In general, the Threatened Actives are not particularly concerned with their appearance. They are the only segment which disagrees that wearing the latest clothing styles makes them feel good. In addition, the Threatened Actives are the segment least likely to believe it's important to look as young as possible.

The Threatened Actives are strongly opposed to plastic surgery. This segment isn't interested in cosmetics that will make them look younger or in products that would return gray hair to its original color. They accept themselves as they are.

Want to continue working

The Threatened Actives, far more than the other three segments, don't believe in retirement and want to continue working. They find the idea of a retirement where they can work if they want, when they want, and for whom they want very appealing.

Car/RV trips most appealing

In relation to intellectual pursuits, the Threatened Actives report that they do not like going to lectures and are not interested in taking courses through the mail or on television.

The Threatened Actives are the most interested in taking long trips by car or RV, not in sitting on the beach.

Love affair with cars

Of the Self segments, the Threatened Actives have the highest level of agreement with being totally dependent on their cars. It is not surprising then that they are very strongly opposed to having older people retested for driver's licenses.

Taking action for safety

The Threatened Actives are becoming increasingly concerned about being crime victims. They are the only Self segment expressing a desire to move to a safer neighborhood. They also believe, far more than the other segments, that older persons should learn how to use a gun.

Prefer their homes

The Threatened Actives are the only segment negative on the idea of living in a condominium. They alone reject retirement communities such as Sun City as the "ideal place to retire."

Not surprisingly, the Threatened Actives agree that they'd really be happy if they could live the rest of their lives in their own home. This statement is, in fact, the one with which they most strongly agree.

Expect discounts, deferential treatment

The Threatened Actives, like the other segments, shop for value. This segment, along with the Financial Positives, buys things that will last a long time.

They are the only Self segment, however, that shops where they can get discounts for seniors. Besides discounts, the Threatened Actives would also appreciate deferential treatment because of their age. Only this segment expects salespeople to be particularly courteous to older customers.

The Threatened Actives would appreciate stores providing more chairs so that shoppers can rest.

Figure 4–7   Residence within Census Regions, 50+ Self Segments

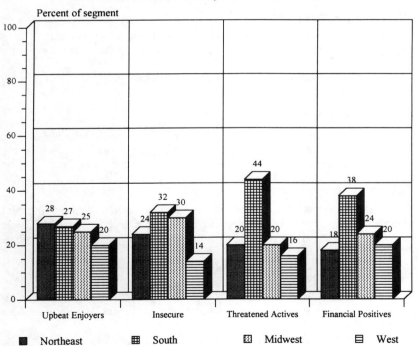

Compared to the other Self segments, more Threatened Actives reside in the South, while more Upbeat Enjoyers are found in the Northeast. More Insecure live in the Midwest.

DEMOGRAPHICS—THE THREATENED ACTIVES

More males than females

Fifty-five percent of the Threatened Actives are male, significantly more than the number of males in the U.S. population over 50 (43 percent). Only in this segment do males outnumber females (see Figure 4–2).

Second youngest Self segment

With a median age of 63 years, compared to 64 years for the over-50 population, the Threatened Actives are the second youngest of the Self segments. While 23 percent of the U.S. population of persons over 50 are over the age of 75, only 20 percent of the Threatened Actives are in this age group (see Figure 4–3).

More married, fewer widowed than total

More of the Threatened Actives are married (63 percent) as compared to the over-50 population (58 percent). On the other hand, only 25 percent are widowed, compared to 30 percent of the U.S. population over 50. In sharp contrast, 44 percent of the Insecure are widowed (see Figure 4–4).

Poorly educated

Along with the Insecure, the Threatened Actives are among the least educated of the Self segments with a median of 11 years of education. Half of those in this segment are high school graduates or less as compared to 45 percent of the U.S. population of persons over 50. In addition, less than a quarter (22 percent) of those in this segment have four years of college or more, compared to almost a third of the Financial Positives and Upbeat Enjoyers (see Figure 4–5).

Low median annual income

With a median income of $19,491, the Threatened Actives have the second lowest annual before-tax household income of the four Self segments. Significantly more Threatened Actives (61 percent) have incomes of less than $30,000 in comparison to all those over 50 (55 percent). Far fewer Upbeat Enjoyers (40 percent) and Financial Positives (39 percent) fall into this income bracket (see Figure 4–6).

Compared to a median of $43,743 for the U.S. population over 50, the Threatened Actives have a median of $33,193 in assets, not including their homes. Their asset level is in contrast to that of the Financial Positives, who have a median of $97,074 in assets.

Southern residents

Compared to 35 percent of the over-50 population, 44 percent of the Threatened Actives reside in the South census region. However, fewer Threatened Actives (20 percent) than any other segment live in the Midwest (see Figure 4–7).

Working more

About as many of the Threatened Actives (60 percent) as the over-50 population (59 percent) have either part-time or full-time jobs (see Figure 4–8).

Working in a variety of occupations

One-fifth of the Threatened Actives are now in or were in professional or technical positions, compared to a quarter of all those over 50. In addition, 13 percent of those in this segment were clerical workers. Ten percent reported being employed in each of the following categories: skilled craftsmen, owners or entrepreneurs, managers or executives, and laborers.

Retiring on par with average

Almost half of the Threatened Actives (48 percent) have retired with no intention of returning to work (see Figure 4–9). This is very close to the percentage of the U.S. population over 50 that has retired (51 percent).

One-third returning to work

Of those who have retired, almost a third (29 percent) have returned to work since retirement, the same percentage of all those over 50 who have done so. The percentage of Threatened Actives who have returned to work is far less than that of the Upbeat Enjoyers (41 percent) (see Figure 4–9).

Homemakers, professionals after retirement

Jobs held by the Threatened Actives who retired and returned to work include homemaker (20 percent), professional or technical (15 percent), clerical (11 percent), and sales (11 percent).

Volunteering less than average

Fewer of the Threatened Actives do volunteer work (39 percent) in comparison to the U.S. population of those over 50 (45 percent) and the Upbeat Enjoyers (57 percent).

Demographic summary

The Threatened Actives segment contains more males than females, as well as more males than any other Self segment. With a median age of 63 years, more Threatened Actives are married and fewer are widowed than those over 50. Of the four Self segments, the Threatened Actives are one of the least educated and have the second lowest median annual income. In addition, their median level of assets is far less than that of the over-50 population. More of the Threatened Actives live in the South than in any other region, and 48 percent of them have retired. Twenty-nine percent of those who retired have returned to work. Those in this segment, who hold or did hold jobs in a variety of occupations, are just as likely as the national sample to work full time or part time, but less likely to volunteer.

THE FINANCIAL POSITIVE SEGMENT

The Financial Positives, the fourth Self segment, make up 28 percent of the over-50 population (see Figure 4–1). This segment feels very financially secure. While the Financial Positives have an affirmative view of life, it's tinged with the realization that the best years of their lives were when they were young.

Successful and optimistic

The Financial Positives consider themselves to be successful people and are optimistic about the future. Those in this segment also feel very lucky and not at all lonely.

The Financial Positives, however, think their memories are not as sharp as they used to be and are somewhat likely to feel that they have already lived through the best years of their lives.

Open to change

The Financial Positives strongly believe that terminally ill patients should be able to stop their own treatment.

They also believe that openness to change is important to their quality of life. Accepting change, the Financial Positives aren't opposed to the legislature passing laws requiring the retesting of older people for driver's licenses.

Financially secure

Although being financially secure is a major concern for the Financial Positives, they are far more secure about their financial future than are the other segments. This statement is, in fact, the one with which the Financial Positives have the highest level of agreement. More than any other Self segment, the Financial Positives believe that they have enough money to live on.

Also more than the other three segments, the Financial Positives believe in planning for a financially secure future and making conservative investments. They will "trust certain financial planners" to advise them or make investments and are the only segment that is positive about doing so.

Concerned with youth and beauty

The Financial Positives believe it is important to look as young as possible and don't believe our society places too much emphasis on youth and beauty.

Those in this segment don't feel that the aging process has been beneficial to their appearance. Feeling less sexy than before, the Financial Positives favor rejuvenating cosmetics and are the segment most likely to be open to plastic surgery as a way to look younger. They are not interested in products that would return gray hair to its original color, however.

Ready for relaxing retirement

The Financial Positives are ready to relax and enjoy life. In comparison to the other segments, they are negative on the idea of a "working retirement." They are happy to retire and are the only segment that has no desire to always continue working at something.

Favor tours

In terms of vacations, the Financial Positives enjoy going on escorted tours, not sitting on the beach. They are somewhat interested in hotels and airlines offering discounts for people over 50.

Safety concerns increasing

Somewhat more concerned than before about falling victim to crimes, the Financial Positives agree, although at a low level, that older people should know how to use guns. However, as they want to stay in their own homes, they are not interested in moving to a "safer neighborhood."

Open to retirement communities

The Financial Positives are the only segment positive to the idea of living in a retirement community, but they more strongly agree that they would be happy to live in their own homes for the rest of their lives.

Won't depend on children

Even when they can no longer care for themselves, the Financial Positives will not rely on their children to care for them.

Shop for value and durability

When shopping, the Financial Positives, much more than the other segments, look for value. They also like to buy things they think will last a long time. They prefer to shop in well-established stores they know. While shopping for good values, they'd appreciate being able to sit down so they can rest. This statement is, incidentally, one with which three of the four segments agree.

DEMOGRAPHICS—THE FINANCIAL POSITIVES

Females are majority

While 58 percent of the over-50 population are female, 55 percent of the Financial Positives are female. The Financial Positives are one of three segments in which females represent the majority (see Figure 4–2).

Second oldest Self segment

The Financial Positives' median age of 64, the same as that for the U.S. population over 50, makes them the second oldest Self segment. Only the Insecure, with a median

**Figure 4–8   Hours of Paid Employment
Per Week, 50+ Self Segments**

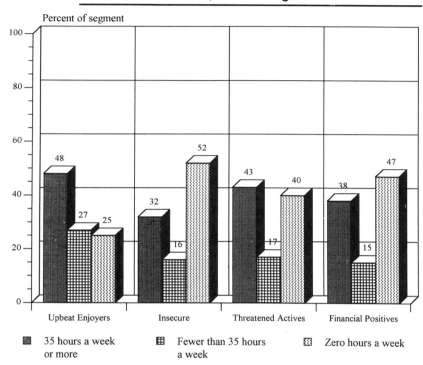

Percent of segment

| | 35 hours a week or more | | Fewer than 35 hours a week | | Zero hours a week |

More Upbeat Enjoyers work full time as compared to other segments. Although they have the lowest household income and fewest assets, more Insecure do not work.

age of 66 years, are older. However, one-fifth of the Financial Positives are between 50 and 55 years old (see Figure 4–3).

Most married, least divorced

The most married of the four Self segments, far more Financial Positives (71 percent) are married compared to the U.S. population over 50 (58 percent). Conversely, significantly fewer Financial Positives (4 percent) than the over-50 population (7 percent) are divorced or separated. In addition, in comparison to 30 percent of all those over 50, only 21 percent of the Financial Positives are widowed (see Figure 4–4).

Highly educated

With a median of 13 years of education, the Financial Positives join the Upbeat Enjoyers as one of the two most highly educated Self segments. Thirty-one percent have had four years of college or more as compared to 26 percent of the U.S. population over 50 (see Figure 4–5).

Wealthiest Self segment

The wealthiest of the four Self segments, the Financial Positives have a median annual pre-tax household income of $37,722 a year. Of those in this segment, 32 percent have annual incomes of more than $50,000. That compares to one in four of the over-50 population and only one in ten of the Insecure (see Figure 4–6). In fact, compared to only 5 percent of the U.S. population over 50, 8 percent of the Financial Positives have median annual household incomes of over $100,000 a year.

In addition, those in this segment have by far the highest asset level of the four Self segments with a median of $97,074 compared to a median of $43,743 for the over-50 population, excluding their homes. The contrast is even more dramatic when compared to the median assets of the Threatened Actives ($33,193) and the Insecure ($24,130).

Figure 4–9   Rate of Retirement and Employment Since Retirement, 50+ Self Segment

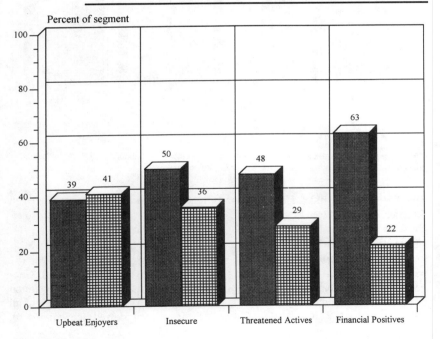

Compared to the other segments, far more Financial Positives have retired with no intention of returning to work. More Upbeat Enjoyers have been employed since retirement.

Living in the South

More of the Financial Positives (38 percent) live in the South census region than in any other. About a quarter of them live in the Midwest and a fifth live in the West. The Financial Positives are least represented in the Northeast (see Figure 4–7).

Working less

Compared to 59 percent of the over-50 population, only 53 percent of the Financial Positives work for pay either part time or full time. In contrast, three-quarters of the Upbeat Enjoyers continue to work at that level (see Figure 4–8).

Professional, managerial positions

Forty-three percent of the Financial Positives segment had or still have a career in a white collar position. Compared to 24 percent of the over-50 population, 27 percent of the Financial Positives worked in a professional or technical position. In addition, in comparison to all those over 50 (12 percent), more Financial Positives (16 percent) held managerial or executive positions. Sixteen percent of those in this segment spent their lives working in clerical jobs.

Taking advantage of retirement

The Financial Positives are the most likely of the Self segments to have retired. In comparison to 51 percent of the total U.S. population over 50, significantly more of the Financial Positives (63 percent) have retired with no intention of returning to work (see Figure 4–9).

Once retired, always retired

In addition to being the most likely to retire, the Financial Positives are the least likely of the Self segments to be employed after retirement. Of those Financial Positives who have retired, only 22 percent, compared to 29 percent of the over-50 population, have returned to work (see Figure 4–9).

More homemakers after retirement

When returning to work after retirement, the Financial Positives have taken such positions as homemaker (22 percent), professional or technical (18 percent), and manager or executive (9 percent). Far fewer Financial Positives (8 percent) returned to clerical positions after retirement than did all those over 50 (13 percent).

Volunteering more

Almost half of the Financial Positives (48 percent) do some volunteer work each week, slightly more than the U.S. population of those over 50 (45 percent), and far more than the Threatened Actives (39 percent) and Insecure (32 percent).

Demographics summary

With a median age of 64 years, the Financial Positives are the most married and least divorced or separated of the four Self segments. Highly educated, the Financial Positives are the wealthiest of the segments in terms of both income and assets. More of the Financial Positives live in the South than in any other region.

The Financial Positives, with careers in professional and managerial positions, are the most likely of the Self segments to retire and the least likely to return to work after retirement. Although fewer Financial Positives as compared to the over-50 population are working for pay, more are volunteering.

FIVE

TRAVEL PLANS

WHAT THEY SPEND

Whether it's sitting on a beach on Sanibel Island, Florida, or climbing the steps to the Sacre Coeur in Paris, mature consumers have shown themselves to be enthusiastic travelers.

Households with travelers over 50 comprise 43 percent of all households, but they take a disproportionate 46 percent of all vacation or pleasure trips. According to the Consumer Expenditures Survey, the $58 billion that mature travelers spent in 1987 on vacation expenses ranging from lodging to gas, trains to entertainment, represented 52 percent of all such U.S. expenditures.

SEGMENTING TODAY'S MATURE TRAVELERS

The Consumer Expenditures Survey also shows that seniors over 65 consume fewer travel-related services compared to those who are 50 to 65. However, Upbeat Enjoyers and Financial Positives who are over 65 continue to travel and spend at rates that exceed the over-65 population. These important distinctions are lost when data is examined only by demographic averages, for example, and not by attitudinal segments.

This chapter affords a detailed examination of our 50+ Self segments as travelers. It explains why each segment travels and outlines different patterns of consumption. This chapter explores the travel needs and motivations of the frequent travelers within the Self segments. International destinations and those within the United States are also reviewed.

In the attitudinal portion of our study, only the Upbeat Enjoyers viewed sitting on a beach as a great vacation idea. Those who sought more discounts for people over 50 were the Insecure and Financial Positives, the two segments most unlike each other in financial resources.

This chapter shows that not all mature travelers want or need the same services. In the past, hotel chains and others have focused on the mature traveler's disabilities. However, not all seniors need or want restaurant menus with large type or telephones with amplifiers.

There are travel experiences and services that the Self segments may not have now but would like to have. Successful travel marketers will focus on satisfying the needs of each Self segment by its attitudes and expectations of travel.

FREQUENCY OF TRAVEL SHAPED BY SEGMENT

Travelers found in two segments

Examining travel by segment shows that consumption is concentrated in two of the four Self segments. Admittedly, being in one of these two affluent segments, the Upbeat Enjoyers and the Financial Positives, is important in determining how frequently one travels and what one pays. The travel needs of each of these two segments are very different, however.

The Financial Positives travel more frequently than do the Upbeat Enjoyers, and they, regardless of age, are the more committed travelers. The Financial Positives, after all, view retirement as part of the good life for which they have planned. Unlike the Upbeat Enjoyers, they do not view work as a part of retirement. More of the Financial Positives than Upbeat Enjoyers look for value in travel and favor all-inclusive packages.

In contrast, the Upbeat Enjoyers are more willing to try exotic locales. For example, more of them, as opposed to the Financial Positives, are planning to visit Asia and Japan in the next five years. There is also a social aspect to the Upbeat Enjoyers' travel that is missing from the profile of the Financial Positives. For example, more Upbeat Enjoyers are influenced by a friend's recommendation on a travel spot. As Upbeat Enjoyers age, however, fewer of them, as opposed to the Financial Positives, take trips.

Favor shorter trips

Just like the rest of us, those over 50 prefer shorter trips. In our study, 45 percent of those over 50 have taken at least one vacation lasting one to four days over the past 12 months. More of the Financial Positives (56 percent) have taken such a brief trip as compared to the Upbeat Enjoyers (52 percent).

In addition, we examined the 50+ Self segments by those who are frequent domestic travelers, that is, those who had made 11 or more domestic trips within the past five years. Those making this number of domestic trips were limited to the upper quartile of our respondents.

We found that many more Financial Positives (72 percent) among frequent domestic travelers as compared to Upbeat Enjoyers (57 percent) had made 11 or more brief domestic trips in the past 12 months.

Longer trips less popular

Only one in four in the population over 50 had taken a trip over 10 days in length during the past 12 months. But one-third of both the Upbeat Enjoyers and Financial Positives had taken such a trip.

Of those persons in the over-50 population who are frequent domestic travelers, more Financial Positives (53 percent), as opposed to Upbeat Enjoyers (48 percent), had taken a long trip. Among these frequent domestic travelers, it's important to note that more of the Financial Positives over 65 had taken a long trip in the past 12 months (64 percent) as compared to those 65 and younger (46 percent). This dramatic contrast supports the idea that attitudes can be more important than a demographic characteristic, such as age, in shaping consumption.

Foreign trips decrease with age

As many people age, fewer of their long trips are to foreign destinations. This tendency is seen in the fact that more Financial Positives 65 and younger (19 percent) plan to visit Western Europe in the next five years than those over 65 (12 percent).

Within the mature population, however, there are those who will continue to make foreign visits after 65. For example, more frequent foreign travelers in the Financial Positive segment are planning a trip to Western Europe in the next five years, including 36 percent of those 65 and younger and 39 percent of those over 65. In our study, frequent foreign travelers were those who had taken two or more foreign trips within the past five years. Regarding such travel, they represent the upper quartile of our respondents.

Making a trip to Western Europe isn't the case with as many frequent foreign travelers within the other affluent segment, the Upbeat Enjoyers. Far fewer of those Upbeat Enjoyers who are over 65 (27 percent) plan to make a trip to Western Europe as compared to those 65 and younger (46 percent). These differences, we believe, rest on attitudes, not demographics.

FACTORS IMPORTANT TO SELECTION

Value, safety, and packages

From a list of 13 items, our respondents were asked to select the three most important that they would consider when deciding where to go on a vacation. These attributes ranged from a videotape of the area to low cost. Among the top factors most often cited within those three were good value, a safe place, a complete package with all costs included, and low cost (see Figure 5–1).

Additional influencers

A friend's recommendation (26 percent) is far more important than advertising (3 percent) as one of the three top influencers on a mature traveler's decision to visit a particular spot. It is important to note, however, that such a recommendation is more important to the Upbeat Enjoyers (33 percent) than to the Financial Positives (29 percent), and less so to the Threatened Actives (21 percent).

As compared to advertising, more of the over-50 population (11 percent) sees information from the media as one of the three most important influencers in making a vacation decision. Among frequent domestic travelers, however, twice as many say that media information influences their decision on where to vacation. This finding suggests that an article in *Travel & Leisure* on the Delta Queen is more potent in attracting persons over 50 to that vacation experience than a glossy advertisement.

**Figure 5–1   Deciding on a Vacation Destination,
All Travelers, 50+ Self Segments**

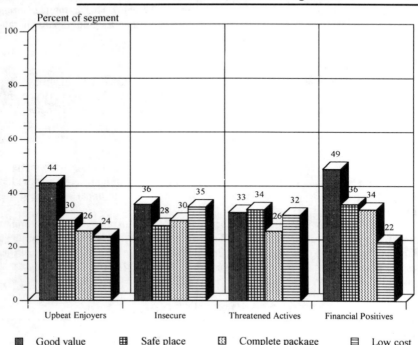

Percent of segment

■ Good value   ⊞ Safe place   ▨ Complete package   ⊟ Low cost

On a multiple-response question on the importance of 13 attributes when deciding on a vacation destination, more Financial Positives report looking for good value, safe places, and complete packages. More Insecure rate low cost as an important attribute.

Important differences appear when we contrast all mature travelers to those who are frequent foreign travelers on the issue of why they select a particular vacation destination. Only two of the reasons most frequently cited by all travelers are also important to frequent foreign travelers: good value and a complete package.

Twice as many Insecure who are frequent foreign travelers rate the criterion of good value as important, compared to all mature travelers. Also of importance to the frequent foreign traveler's selection process are the appearance of a destination being very different from their home area and the recommendation by a friend (see Figure 5–2).

Using relationships to promote

The strength of a friend's recommendation could be developed in promotions that include bringing a friend along at half price or earning accommodations for a friend

Figure 5–2   Deciding on a Vacation Destination, Frequent Foreign Travelers, 50+ Self Segments

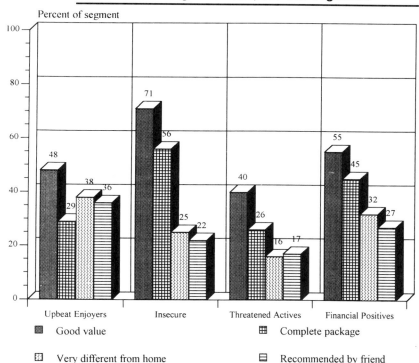

Percent of segment

Upbeat Enjoyers   Insecure   Threatened Actives   Financial Positives

🔲 Good value   ⊞ Complete package

▣ Very different from home   ⊟ Recommended by friend

On a multiple-response question on the importance of 13 attributes when deciding on a vacation destination, more frequent foreign travelers in the Upbeat Enjoyers segment report looking for a place very different from home. More Insecure want good values and complete packages.

through one's own stay. Such programs are built on paying attention to individual travelers and building a relationship with them.

VACATION PREFERENCES

Taking an escorted tour

The 50+ study found that 19 percent of persons over 50 had taken an escorted tour in the previous five years; we also discovered differences between segments in this regard (see Figure 5–3).

Of those frequent foreign travelers in the over-50 population, 39 percent have taken an escorted tour over the past five years. However, frequent foreign travelers within the Upbeat Enjoyers segment (69 percent) who are over 65 have taken far more escorted tours as compared to Financial Positives (60 percent) over 65.

Cruises have broad appeal

One out of seven of the population over 50 has gone on a cruise in the past five years. Differences among the attitudinal segments become more important when many demographic characteristics fail to distinguish cruise goers. For example, cruises appeal equally to those 65 and younger as to those over 65 and to virtually the same percentage of females as males. Among frequent foreign travelers, however, far more Financial Positives (44 percent) as compared to Upbeat Enjoyers (37 percent) had gone on a cruise in the past five years (see Figure 5–4). Financial Positives in this category who are also over 65 have the highest cruise participation (48 percent).

**Figure 5–3   Types of Vacation Trips,
All Travelers, 50+ Self Segments**

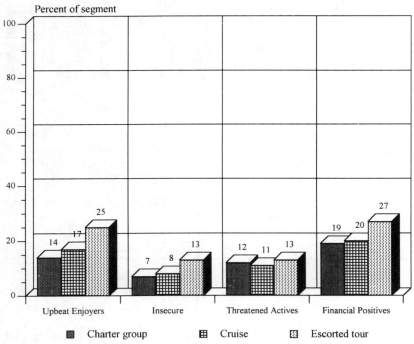

On a multiple-response question on the frequency of taking three types of group trips in the past five years, more Financial Positives report going on such trips.

To increase the success of their promotions, cruise marketers have to be able to identify and reach the Financial Positive segment through both media and direct marketing. Beyond strategies based on cost, marketers for cruise lines must understand what motivates the Financial Positives and construct packages and promotions that focus on those interests.

Staying at a hotel

Our 50+ study shows that of the pleasure trips taken over the past 12 months by persons over 50, 47 percent include a stay in a motel or hotel. Hotel stays are more typical of the Upbeat Enjoyers (59 percent) and Financial Positives (58 percent) than the Insecure (33 percent).

**Figure 5–4 Types of Vacation Trips,
Frequent Foreign Travelers,
50+ Self Segments**

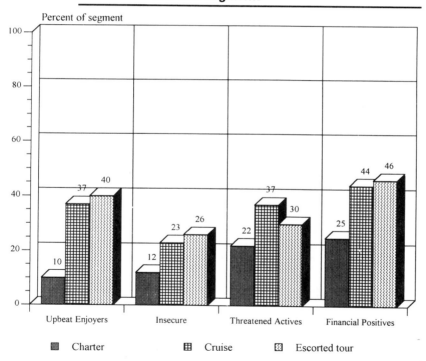

On a multiple-response question on the frequency of taking three types of group trips over the past five years, more frequent foreign travelers in the Financial Positives segment, compared to the other segments, report having gone on all three. Frequent foreign travelers have taken two or more foreign trips in the past five years.

Price paid for room

On a pleasure trip, the median price paid for a hotel or motel room differs by segment. The population over 50 pays a median of $54.87 for a hotel room, compared to an average rate of $58.91 in 1991 for the general population. The Insecure pay the least: $50.58. In contrast, the Upbeat Enjoyers pay far more: $60.59. Although they are the wealthiest segment, the value-oriented Financial Positives pay closer to the national median for people over 50: $56.49.

GETTING TO VACATION SPOTS

Using their own cars

When traveling for pleasure, 80 percent of those over 50 always or frequently use their own car to get to their destination. Because fewer Insecure own a car, it isn't surprising that only 76 percent of them always or frequently use their own cars to get to their vacation spot (see Figure 5–5). In fact, when only frequent domestic travelers among the Insecure are considered, use of their own cars increases (see Figure 5–6).

RV: taking to the road

Of all recreational vehicle (RV) trips, 72 percent are made by those over 50. Of the population over 50, 10 percent usually stay in an RV while traveling. More of the Threatened Actives (11 percent) and Financial Positives (12 percent) prefer this form of accommodation.

Come fly with me

While 84 percent of those over 50 use an airplane to get to their vacation spot, more of the Upbeat Enjoyers (90 percent) and Financial Positives (88 percent) do so. The heaviest users, those who always or frequently use an airplane, are, however, the Upbeat Enjoyers. In contrast to the Financial Positives (47 percent), more of the Upbeat Enjoyers (54 percent) always or frequently fly (see Figure 5–5).

In rating 12 attributes relating to airline service, the five designated as very important by most respondents, including frequent foreign and domestic travelers, are a good safety record, more direct flights, taking off on time, attractive deals, and convenient take-off times. These attributes sound very much like those desired by persons under 50.

Senior services less desired

In our study, those airline service attributes designed for older travelers got lower ratings. A senior travel program was rated as very important by only one-third of those over 50. Only one out of seven of those over 50 thought that receiving extra attention because of their age was very important.

When these age-specific services are examined by segment, however, it is apparent that more of the Insecure, the segment that travels least by air, want such services. For

**Figure 5–5   Transportation Used,
All Travelers, 50+ Self Segments**

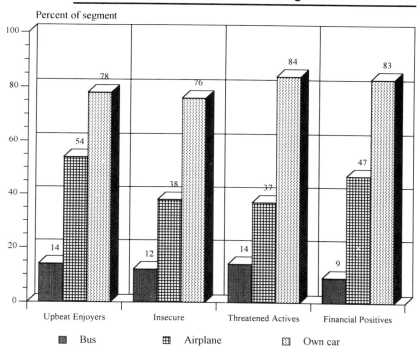

Percent of segment

On a multiple-response question on the frequency of using six modes of transportation to get to vacation destinations, more Threatened Actives and Financial Positives report "always" or "frequently" using their own cars. More Upbeat Enjoyers fly with such frequency.

example, fewer Upbeat Enjoyers (26 percent), the segment that flies the most, are interested in a senior travel program, as compared to the Insecure (38 percent).

Infrequent users most demanding

Responding to data from traditional research that reports averages, companies and organizations often shape products and services giving undue weight to persons whose own motivations and needs make them generally demanding. In many cases, what these consumers ask for is related far more to their own personal situation than to needs related to the product or service. When these demanding customers are also infrequent users, the folly of paying undue attention to their demands is evident.

In attribute after attribute, from attractive deals to more direct flights, the Insecure want more from airlines in terms of service than the other segments, and yet they fly least frequently. The Insecure, we should remember, are an unhappy group that feels

Figure 5–6   Transportation Used, Frequent Domestic Travelers, 50+ Self Segments

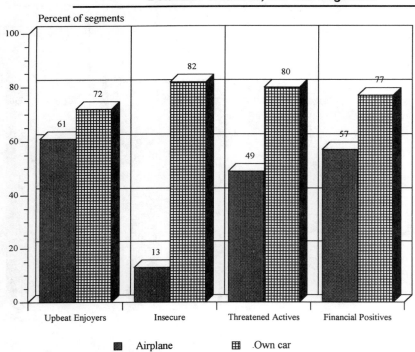

On a multiple-response question on the frequency of using six modes of transportation to get to vacation destinations, more frequent domestic travelers in the Insecure and Threatened Active segments drive their own cars.

as if the best years of their lives are behind them. An airline could exhaust its marketing resources catering to the needs of those it can never satisfy because their demands are driven far more by their personal situation than by the experience of travel.

DESTINATIONS

U.S. regions visited

The least visited region in the United States is the Midwest. Only 30 percent of those persons over 50 have visited the Midwest in the past five years. However, more Financial Positives, who live primarily in the South and West, have done so.

Although more of them live in the Midwest, fewer Insecure have traveled in the Midwest than the other segments (22 percent) and fewer of them intend to do so in the next five years (14 percent).

Visiting the South, West, and East

In considering visits to the South, West, and East, a highly consistent pattern emerges. About 40 percent of those over 50 have visited each region in the past five years. Secondly, over half of the Upbeat Enjoyers and Financial Positives have visited each of these three regions over the past five years. About 40 percent of both the Financial Positives and Upbeat Enjoyers say they will be visiting these regions again over the next five years.

While recognizing the tendency for someone who lives in a particular region to vacation there, this is not always the case. For example, fewer Upbeat Enjoyers live in the South, whereas more of the Financial Positives do. Yet virtually the same percentages of them visited the South in the past five years.

Travel outside continental United States

Over the past five years, the four most popular destinations outside the continental United States for those over 50 have been Alaska, Hawaii, Canada, and the Caribbean. Of those over 50, 22 percent have visited Canada. The Caribbean, Hawaii, and Alaska have each been visited by 15 percent.

One in five Upbeat Enjoyers and Financial Positives has visited Alaska or Hawaii over the past five years. Among frequent domestic travelers, Alaska or Hawaii has been visited by more Financial Positives (39 percent) than Upbeat Enjoyers (31 percent).

Canada a popular destination

Canada has been visited by almost one in four of the over-50 population in the past five years. However, even more of the Upbeat Enjoyers (30 percent) and Financial Positives (28 percent) have done so. In fact, among frequent domestic travelers, slightly more than half of the Upbeat Enjoyers and Financial Positives have visited Canada over the past five years (53 and 50 percent respectively). One in six frequent domestic travelers in these two segments has made from three to ten or more trips to Canada over the past five years.

One in ten visit Europe

Western Europe has been visited by one in ten of those over 50 in the last five years. More of the Upbeat Enjoyers (17 percent) and Financial Positives (15 percent) have completed this trip. But far more male Upbeat Enjoyers (64 percent) who are frequent foreign travelers have made such a trip as compared to male Financial Positives (50 percent). In our view, between segments with similar financial resources, diverging attitudes toward travel help to shape these types of differences.

Respondents to the 50+ study were also asked about their travel to seven additional, more unusual or remote, destinations. For example, a small percentage of mature travelers had visited the former Soviet Union (1 percent), Eastern Europe (5 percent), or South America (4 percent) over the past five years.

Again we find that more male Upbeat Enjoyers who are frequent foreign travelers have visited these more unusual locations compared to male Financial Positives. For example, more of them (22 percent) had visited Eastern Europe compared to the male Financial Positives (15 percent).

Next five years

Far more Upbeat Enjoyers than Financial Positives say they intend to visit these more unusual places in the next five years. Just as we don't believe that financial resources account for the difference in travel patterns between the Upbeat Enjoyers and Financial Positives, we don't see age as a critical differentiator.

Both segments are similar in age: the Upbeat Enjoyers have a median age of 62, whereas the Financial Positives' median age is 64. But slightly more Upbeat Enjoyers (8 percent) say that they plan to visit Asia or Japan in the next five years as compared to Financial Positives (6 percent).

In terms of travel planned for the next five years, the Insecure and Threatened Actives are, at best, average consumers and, at worst, underconsumers. In fact, one in ten of both the Insecure and Threatened Actives plans no vacations at all over the next five years as compared to one in 20 of the Upbeat Enjoyers and Financial Positives.

Over the next five years, more frequent foreign travelers among the Upbeat Enjoyers will visit the British Isles and Western Europe as compared to frequent foreign travelers among the Financial Positives (see Figure 5–7).

CONCLUSION

European travel boards, as well as every state's travel commission, eagerly await the appearance of the mature traveler in their lands. While demographics are important, segments clearly differ in their expectations of travel. Those who understand what motivates different attitudinal segments within the mature market will be most successful in attracting them.

Demographic characteristics, such as age or income, do not totally determine what the mature traveler wants. Significant differences exist within the group of travelers over 50 who are healthy enough to travel and have the time and money to do so. Getting the biggest return on a marketing investment means targeting beyond those who *should* be interested in a travel offering and reaching those who actually *are*.

REFERENCES

U.S. Bureau of Labor Statistics, *Consumer Expenditure Survey 1988-89,* Bulletin 2383, Washington, D.C.

McDowell, Edwin, "Look and You'll Find Lodging Discounts," *Star Tribune,* January 3, 1993.

"RV Facts," *Mature Market Report,* March 1989.

**Figure 5–7   Vacation Destinations for Next Five Years,
Frequent Foreign Travelers,
50+ Self Segments**

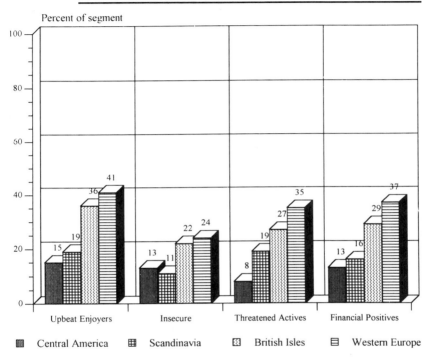

On a multiple-response question on the intention of visiting 17 vacation destinations in the next five years, more frequent foreign travelers in the Upbeat Enjoyers segment report planning to visit three of these four destinations.

SIX

CARS AND AUTOMOBILE CLUBS

GIVING UP WHEELS

After being ticketed for causing two major accidents in three months, the 78-year-old man insists that the accidents are not his fault. He responds angrily to a suggestion that he give up driving: "I'd be nothing if I couldn't drive."

From our first driver's license to the purchase of our last car, the automobile remains a potent symbol for freedom, fantasy, sexuality, and mobility. A great deal of our own identity is given up when we finally hang up our keys around 85, the age at which the majority of Americans have ceased to drive. At that age, only 22 percent have a valid driver's license, compared to the 75 percent who had one ten years previously.

ATTITUDES TOWARD CARS AND DRIVING

Given the importance of the automobile in our lives, it's no wonder that one segment in particular, the Threatened Actives, strongly disagrees with the idea of retesting older people for driver's licenses. Far more of the Threatened Actives (47 percent) are strongly against retesting, compared to the population over 50 (22 percent). The Threatened Actives also feel most strongly that they are totally dependent on their car to get around.

Cars are an integral part of our lives, and consumers over 50 are also an important market for manufacturers of automobiles, especially American ones. In this chapter we'll explore which brands of cars are driven by the Self segments. And, more importantly, we will outline which car brands are gaining market share among mature consumers at the expense of others. Our study supports the fact that advertising to the mature market is paying off for some car manufacturers. Automobile club managers will see how those in one female subsegment are overconsumers of their services.

Car sales to over 50 market

As little as ten years ago, those over 50 represented only one in four new car sales. In 1990 mature consumers bought 41 percent of new cars. In 1990, the latest year for which information is available, new car sales to those over 50 totaled $60 billion.

Car manufacturers have to focus on this market's needs. As their numbers increase over the next several years, the over-50 market's importance to car manufacturers will escalate tremendously. U.S. car manufacturers in particular should pay attention to those over 50 because they purchase 43 percent of all domestic cars.

By the year 2000, sales of cars and trucks to those over 50 will increase from 33 to 36 percent. By then, expenditures on repairs and maintenance by those over 50 will represent 39 percent of all sales for these services, an increase from 36 percent.

WHO OWNS A CAR?

Of those over 50 in the U.S. population, 93 percent own a car. Within the 50+ Self segments, fewer Insecure own a car (89 percent) as compared to Financial Positives (97 percent). Unlike any other Self segment, however, fewer male Insecure (85 percent) own a car as compared to the females in that segment (91 percent).

Although they are financially comfortable, increased age reduces the number of Upbeat Enjoyers who own a car far more than it does for the other Self segments. After the age of 65 fewer of the Upbeat Enjoyers (83 percent) own a car as compared to those 65 and younger (97 percent). The drop among the other segments averages about 10 percent. In contrast, as the Financial Positives age, car ownership erodes the least: from 99 to 94 percent.

Only one car

In the over-50 population, 54 percent have only one car. However, this is more true of the Insecure (69 percent). The percentage of one-car ownership increases to 79 percent when only Insecure over 65 are considered.

Multiple car ownership

Owning two cars is highest among the Financial Positives. More of them (45 percent) have two cars as compared to persons over 50 (35 percent). However, more Upbeat Enjoyers have three or more cars. As compared to the Upbeat Enjoyers (15 percent), fewer of those over 50 have three or more cars (12 percent).

Male Upbeat Enjoyers own multiple cars

The male Upbeat Enjoyers own the greatest number of cars of any of the subsegments. In this subsegment, 69 percent own more than one car and 23 percent own three or more. While 66 percent of the male Financial Positives own more than one car, only 15 percent own three or more.

Two cars for female Financial Positives

In every segment, males own more cars than do females. However, more female Financial Positives (40 percent) own two cars than any other female subsegment. For example, only 32 percent of the more affluent female Upbeat Enjoyers own two cars.

MILES DRIVEN PER WEEK

Upbeat Enjoyers drive more

The median number of miles driven each week by the over-50 population is 73. The Upbeat Enjoyers drive a median of 93 miles a week as compared to the Insecure, who only drive 53 miles a week. Within the Upbeat Enjoyer segment, males drive the most. The median miles driven per week by male Upbeat Enjoyers is 141 as compared to 66 miles driven by female Upbeat Enjoyers (see Figure 6–1).

One explanation for the fact that the male Upbeat Enjoyers drive an average of 20 miles a day is that more of them currently work full time. Almost half (48 percent) of the Upbeat Enjoyers work 35 or more hours per week as compared to those over 50 (40 percent).

Males outdistance females

Males drive an average of 87 percent more miles per week than females. These dramatic differences in miles driven per week could signal a diminished quality of life for females over 50. With their mobility curtailed, they may withdraw from activities or find themselves far more dependent on others for transportation.

Female Financial Positives put in the miles

Considering their high level of multiple car ownership and auto club membership, it's not surprising that female Financial Positives drive a median of 71 miles per week, more than females in all other segments (see Figure 6–1). The number of miles driven each week by the female Financial Positives is virtually identical to that driven by the population over 50: 73 miles.

AGE OF CARS

In considering the age of the respondents' newest cars, we created three categories. Newest cars range from 1990 to 1992. Cars in the middle-age range are those models from 1986 to 1989. The very oldest cars are those from 1985 or older. These very oldest cars reflect the average age of a car driven in the United States today: eight years.

Insecure drive oldest cars

The Insecure are the most likely to be driving a car that is in the very oldest category. More Insecure (48 percent) are driving a car in this category as compared to those over 50 (36 percent). In contrast, more Financial Positives and Upbeat Enjoyers (29 and 27 percent respectively) are driving 1990 to 1992 model cars as compared to those over 50 (22 percent) (see Figure 6–2).

Of the female Insecure, 52 percent are driving cars in the very oldest category. There is virtually no difference between the percentage of male and female Financial Positives who drive these very oldest cars (26 and 27 percent respectively). However, a far more dramatic difference exists between male Upbeat Enjoyers (23 percent) and

Figure 6–1   Median Miles Driven Per Week, Males and Females, 50+ Self Segments

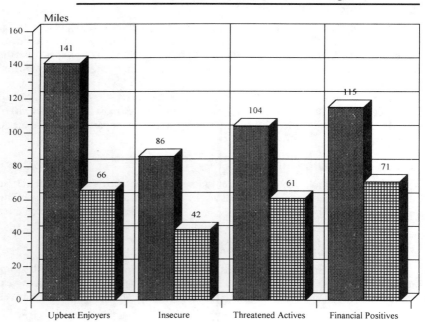

Male Upbeat Enjoyers are driving the most miles per week. Among the female subsegments, the female Financial Positives are driving the greatest number of miles.

female Upbeat Enjoyers (39 percent) on this point. Because they drive the greatest number of miles per week, many male Upbeat Enjoyers probably wouldn't own older cars.

Newest cars driven by two segments

More male Upbeat Enjoyers and male Financial Positives (31 percent each) own cars in the newest category as compared to those over 50 (22 percent). Then, too, more Financial Positives 65 and younger (35 percent) drive a car in the newest category as compared to the population over 50. However, ownership of cars in the newest category decreases even for Financial Positives over 65 (21 percent).

Figure 6–2   Year of Newest Car Owned, 50+ Self Segments

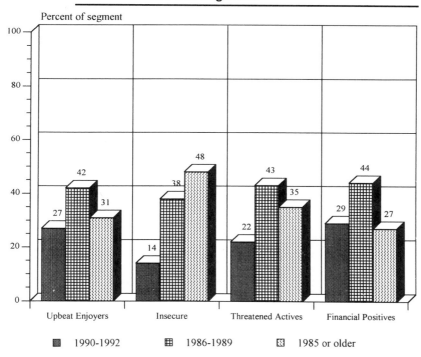

Percent of segment

| | 1990-1992 | | 1986-1989 | | 1985 or older |

Of the four Self segments, more Financial Positives own the newest cars, as well as cars in the 1986-1989 category. More Insecure own cars made in 1985 or before.

WHAT ARE THEY DRIVING?

Own American brands

When asked about the brand of the newest car they owned, the five brands of cars most frequently cited by persons over 50 are Ford, Chevrolet, Oldsmobile, Buick, and Dodge. The newest car owned by almost one in five persons over 50 is a Ford. In contrast, only one in 20 owns a Dodge. Perhaps the mature consumers' loyalty to Ford exists, in part, because this car manufacturer has been targeting them for ten years through "product design, advertising, sales and service," according to an article in *Ad Forum.*

Fords, Chevrolets, and Oldsmobiles are especially to be found in the garages of the Threatened Actives. One out of every four female Threatened Actives drives a Ford. Although Oldsmobile may tout that it's "not your father's Oldsmobile," more Upbeat

Enjoyers over 65 (16 percent) drive an Oldsmobile as compared to the over-50 population (11 percent).

Allure of foreign-made cars

When one combines the Upbeat Enjoyers' ownership of European cars with those made in Asia, we find that a quarter of the Upbeat Enjoyers own a foreign car. More Upbeat Enjoyers (19 percent) own a Japanese or other Asian car as compared to those in the over-50 population (13 percent).

In addition, more Upbeat Enjoyers (6 percent) own a European car as compared to the population over 50 (3 percent). At the present time, ownership of foreign-made cars is slightly higher among male Upbeat Enjoyers in contrast to females. However, as many female Upbeat Enjoyers drive a Honda as do males (5 percent each).

Toyota and Volvo should take note that among the over-50 population, the Upbeat Enjoyers are the least likely to own an American car and the most likely to own a foreign car. Sales of imports to those over 50 have increased at a much faster rate than for those under 50 over the past several years. We believe that it's the Upbeat Enjoyers who have been leading this charge.

Luxury car sales

Almost half (48 percent) of all luxury cars are purchased by someone over 50. More of the Financial Positives (9 percent), as compared to the population over 50 (5 percent), own a Cadillac. When one considers only male Financial Positives, however, the percentage who currently own a Cadillac as their newest car increases to 11 percent.

BUYING A NEW CAR

Within the over-50 population, one in five intends to buy a new, unused car either this year or next. This percentage is the same as that in our 1989 50+ study. Based solely on this intention to buy, we estimate that 6.5 million cars will be sold to persons over 50 in 1993. On a more conservative note, if 10 million new cars are sold in the United States in 1993, purchases of these cars by persons over 50, who account for 41 percent of new car sales, would generate $71 billion in sales.

Sales largely in two segments

Sales of new autos will be concentrated among the Upbeat Enjoyers and Financial Positives, nearly one-quarter of whom say that they will be buying a car in the one- or two-year time frame (see Figure 6–3). Furthermore, buying intention is higher among male Upbeat Enjoyers and male Financial Positives (30 and 27 percent respectively), more of whom say that they will buy a car than their female counterparts (see Figure 6–4).

Surprisingly, even 27 percent of the male Threatened Actives intend to buy a new car within the next two years (see Figure 6–4). Far fewer new car sales will be among the Insecure.

No new car purchase planned

One-third of those over 50 say they never intend to buy a new, unused car. An even greater percentage of Insecure (48 percent) say that they do not ever intend to buy such a car (see Figure 6–3). In all segments, more males as compared to females will drive a new car off the lot this year or next (see Figure 6–4).

Equal percentages of male and female Financial Positives say they will not be buying a new car (21 percent each). That female Financial Positives hold their own on this point parallels other findings we have presented regarding the importance of automobile ownership to them.

Future brand choice

Of those who say that they intend to purchase a new car in the next year or two, more of those over 50 would buy a Ford (17 percent) than any other American brand.

Figure 6–3   Buying a New Car, 50+ Self Segments

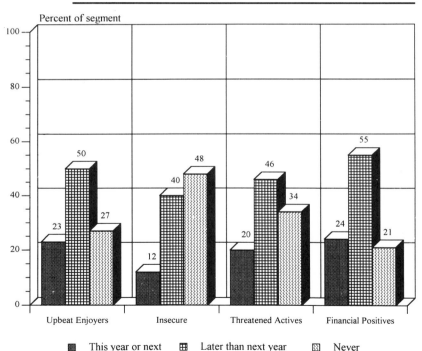

Compared to the other segments, more Financial Positives and Upbeat Enjoyers plan to buy a new car. More Insecure will never buy a new car.

**Figure 6–4   Buying a New Car,
Males and Females, 50+ Self Segments**

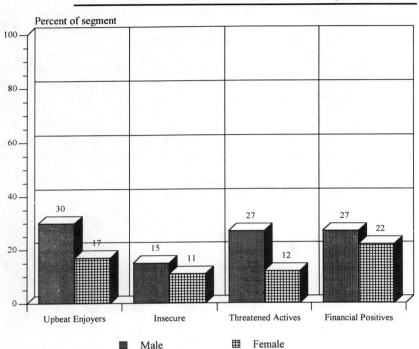

Percent of segment

Male   Female

Compared to males in other segments, more male Upbeat Enjoyers plan to buy a new car this year or next. Among the female subsegments, more female Financial Positives plan to do so.

More than the population over 50, the Threatened Actives will buy Fords (21 percent). At this time, more mature consumers own a Ford (18 percent) as their newest car than any other brand of car, foreign or domestic.

Fewer persons over 50 who intend to buy a new car at some time say they will buy a Chevrolet or Oldsmobile compared to the percentage of those who now own these brands of cars. However, more Insecure over-65 intend to remain loyal to Oldsmobile. More of these in this segment (18 percent) as compared to the population over 50 (9 percent) say that they will buy an Oldsmobile as their next new car.

Buick leading the way

Buick should increase its market share among those over 50, particularly with the Upbeat Enjoyers. At the present time, Buick is the fourth most frequently owned car brand among the mature population (9 percent). However, Buick is the second most frequently cited new car choice (14 percent) among those over 50 who intend to buy a new car at some future time.

Buick has picked up the most converts among the Upbeat Enjoyers over 65. One out of five of those in this subsegment who intend to buy a car at some time say that their new car choice would be a Buick, as compared to one out of ten for Upbeat Enjoyers overall.

According to John Dabels, former General Motors' Consumer Products and Services Commissioner, "Buick market share among seniors has helped it become the only domestic manufacturer to have a market share increase in the last few years." While Buick has not specifically targeted the Upbeat Enjoyer segment, Dabels believes that "Buick is as advanced as anybody in terms of recognizing senior buyers."

The success that Buick is enjoying with mature car buyers is part of a well-planned effort. A comprehensive internal program is paired with such external efforts as intergenerational commercials, Buick's sponsorship of the national Paul Harvey radio program, and advertisements in *Modern Maturity*. In addition, Buick offers a $400 discount coupon on a new Buick to mature buyers.

Opting for luxury

Six percent of those over 50 say that they will buy a Cadillac, with 10 percent of the Financial Positives reflecting this view. However, more male Financial Positives (12 percent) say that their new car would be a Cadillac.

Buying a new import

Although 25 percent of the Upbeat Enjoyers now drive a foreign car, 29 percent intend to buy such a car at some time in the future. In contrast, the Threatened Actives are least likely to purchase a new car from a foreign manufacturer.

While male Upbeat Enjoyers continue to favor a variety of foreign cars slightly more than their female counterparts, Toyota's advertising to mature women appears to be working. The television advertisement that comes to mind features a group of mature women enjoying the power in a Camry's engine as they enter a freeway.

At the present time, 6 percent of the female Upbeat Enjoyers own a Toyota as their newest car. Of those who intend to buy a new car sometime in the future, however, 9 percent of the female Upbeat Enjoyers would purchase a Toyota.

AUTO CLUB MEMBERSHIP

Overall, 69 percent of all persons over 50 are members of an automobile club. According to the American Automobile Association (AAA), only 45 percent of the entire U.S. population are, by contrast, members of an auto club.

AAA is the auto club that dominates the mature market, capturing one-third of all persons over 50 as members. The percentage of membership in other clubs, such as Amoco's or that from Allstate Insurance, is in the single digits.

In addition, AAA is favored even more by certain Self segments. Membership in this auto club is higher among the Upbeat Enjoyers (35 percent) and Financial

Positives (38 percent) as compared to the population over 50 (32 percent). The subsegment with the highest membership in AAA is the female Financial Positives (45 percent).

Competing clubs appeal to Threatened Active

Although the Threatened Actives want to continue driving and say their cars are important to them, this segment is not higher in auto club membership than the over-50 population. With only an average level of membership in AAA, the Threatened Actives display a greater tendency than the other segments to be members of other auto clubs.

For example, automobile clubs run by Allstate Insurance and Amoco attract Threatened Actives. It may be that the Threatened Actives find AAA more expensive than alternative clubs, or they may prefer to receive such coverage from another source.

Club delivers important services

Of the services received by the members of a travel club who are over 50, road service or towing is the most frequently cited (92 percent). More Threatened Actives and Upbeat Enjoyers (94 percent each) rely on such service. Free maps or an atlas is used by more of the Financial Positives and Upbeat Enjoyers (82 percent each) as compared to those over 50 who are auto club members (77 percent). Trip planning is used by more Upbeat Enjoyers (83 percent) and Financial Positives (82 percent) than those in the over-50 population (74 percent). While 51 percent of those auto club members over 50 receive accidental death or dismemberment coverage, more of the Threatened Actives do so (56 percent) (see Figure 6–5).

Use of discount coupons for travel

More of the Upbeat Enjoyers (41 percent) and Financial Positives (40 percent) who are auto club members continue to seek good values by using discount coupons supplied by the travel club as compared to auto club members within the population over 50 (36 percent). Far fewer of the segment with the lowest household income, the Insecure, use such discount coupons (30 percent).

Perhaps the Insecure don't use these coupons because they are the segment least likely to stay at a hotel when traveling. And when they do stay at a hotel, they pay the lowest amount for a room. It may be that even with a coupon, hotel rooms promoted by an auto club are still too expensive for them.

What attracts female Financial Positives?

We've seen that more female Financial Positives (82 percent) are members of an auto club as compared to the over-50 population (69 percent). This may be for a number of reasons. Compared to those over 50 (80 percent), more of them (85 percent) always or frequently use their own cars to get to their vacation destinations. In addition, compared to females in the other Self segments, female Financial Positives drive more miles per week.

Figure 6–5 Auto Club Services, 50+ Self Segments

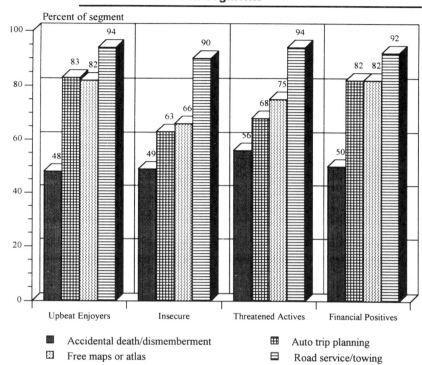

Percent of segment

Upbeat Enjoyers — Insecure — Threatened Actives — Financial Positives

■ Accidental death/dismemberment ⊞ Auto trip planning
▨ Free maps or atlas ⊟ Road service/towing

On a multiple-response question listing six services offered by automobile clubs, more Threatened Actives who are members of such a club receive accidental death or dismemberment insurance. Insecure who are members tend to receive fewer services.

The age of their cars may also influence them to pay for an auto club membership. While 27 percent of them drive cars in the newest category, the same percentage drive cars in the very oldest category.

And the auto club of choice for the female Financial Positives is AAA. While 32 percent of the population over 50 belongs to AAA and 30 percent of male Financial Positives do so, 45 percent of the female Financial Positives are members.

Female Financial Positives use more services

Not only are more of the female Financial Positives members, but they consume more auto club services as compared to members in the over-50 population. For example, while 51 percent of the over-50 population who are auto club members purchase accidental death and dismemberment insurance, 55 percent of the female Financial Positives do.

In the female Financial Positive subsegment, 31 percent get their airline and railroad tickets from their auto club in contrast to 25 percent of auto club members in the over-50 population.

More female Financial Positives receive the remaining three auto club services, including a free atlas or map, at a rate higher than the over-50 population. The same percentage of this subsegment (91 percent) receives road service and towing, as does the population over 50 who are auto club members.

Because they are especially good customers and a significant portion of their mature membership, auto clubs, and most of all AAA, should pay particular attention to keeping female Financial Positives happy.

CONCLUSION

Attitudinal preferences are clearly seen in the brands of cars purchased by each of the four Self segments. Besides loyalty to a certain brand of car, we also see the Upbeat Enjoyers clearly favoring foreign cars and the Threatened Actives and Financial Positives preferring to buy American.

U.S. car manufacturers must do more than simply target those over 50 as a homogeneous group. They must hone their sights on converting the Upbeat Enjoyers to their brands and solidifying their position with the other segments.

Auto clubs should develop more services and products that can be marketed to the female Financial Positives. Females in this segment rely on their auto club for a variety of services now. This relationship should be developed.

REFERENCES

Ambry, Margaret, *Consumer Power: How Americans Spend Their Money,* Chicago: Probus Publishing Co., 1992.

"Buick Gains Market Share with Mature Market Focus, Corporate Reorganization," *Maturity Market Perspectives,* November/December 1991, pp. 1, 8.

Consumer Expenditure Survey, 1988.

Dabels, John, "Satisfying Seniors' Preferences Benefits All Consumers, GM Finds," *Mature Market Report,* May 1992, pp. 1, 4.

Dychtwald, Ken, and Joe Flower, *Age Wave,* Los Angeles: Jeremy P. Tarcher, 1989, p. 268.

"Ford Reshapes Cars to Fit Growing Elderly Market," *Ad Forum,* September 1983, p. 23.

"Mature America in the 1990s," special report from *Modern Maturity* magazine and The Roper Organization, 1992, p. 27.

Motor Vehicle Manufacturers Association of the United States (MVMA), *Facts & Figures 1992.*

Vierck, Elizabeth, *Fact Book on Aging*, Santa Barbara: ABC-CLIO, Inc., 1990, p. 68.

SEVEN

RETIREMENT AND ITS FINANCING

THE THIRD AGE

A group of 70-year-olds sits next to a pool in Sun City, Arizona, slathering on sun-tan lotion after a game of shuffleboard. Is this retirement in the United States? Or is retirement worrying about whether the heat is going to be turned off because the utility bill hasn't been paid?

Does retirement in this country mean vacationing in Scotland or using food stamps for groceries? Does it begin with 50-year-olds who are able, through careful planning, to retire, never to work again? Or 80-year-olds who put in full days at their offices every day?

In this chapter we will look at the Self segments and their attitudes toward retirement and work. Next, we'll examine when they began planning for retirement. The financial sources for their retirement will be reviewed, as well as their attitudes toward risk in investments and their use of financial advisors.

Median age at retirement

For the population over 50, the median retirement age is 61—as it is with the Upbeat Enjoyers and the Threatened Actives. The Insecure retire at a slightly older median age of 63. The Financial Positives, on the other hand, retire at a median age of 60.

Retiring from work

Slightly more than half (51 percent) of those over 50 have retired with no intention of returning to work. At 66 and above, the number of those who have done so rises to 71 percent.

However, dramatic differences exist among the Self segments regarding rates of retirement. Fewer Upbeat Enjoyers over 50 have retired with no intention of returning to work (39 percent) compared to the Financial Positives (63 percent). The Insecure (50 percent) and Threatened Actives (48 percent) are closer to the national norm.

Upbeat Enjoyers like to work

Although the median age of the Upbeat Enjoyers is slightly lower (62 years) versus that of the Financial Positives (64 years), we believe that differences between these two segments regarding whether or not they have retired can be explained by their attitudes.

In the attitudinal portion of the questionnaire, the Upbeat Enjoyers agreed that they don't believe in retirement and always want to "work at something." This is an attitude shared even more strongly by the Threatened Actives. In contrast, the Financial Positives were very negative on continuing to work in retirement. The Financial Positives also disagreed with the idea of a flexible work arrangement in retirement, a statement toward which the Upbeat Enjoyers were most positive.

RETURNING TO WORK

Even after retirement, a sizable portion (29 percent) of the over-50 population returns to paid employment. Paralleling their attitude toward retirement, far more Upbeat Enjoyers over 65 (44 percent) have returned to work after retiring. The second highest rate of returning to work—40 percent—is seen among the Insecure over 65. In contrast, far fewer Financial Positives over 65 (22 percent) have taken up this option (see Figure 7–1).

Reasons for returning to work

A number of reasons motivated retirees to return to paid employment. Of the four selections in a multiple choice question addressing why they had returned to work after retirement, the reasons most often selected by our respondents were keeping busy and financial need (52 percent each). However, there were great differences between the Self segments regarding their motivations.

Far more of the Upbeat Enjoyers (66 percent) had returned to work because they enjoy working, as compared to the population over 50 (46 percent). For the Insecure the two primary reasons for returning to work were to keep busy (67 percent) and financial need (71 percent). In contrast, only 31 percent of the Financial Positives had returned to work because of financial need.

When this data is examined by gender and age, additional disparities are revealed. While 48 percent of the male Upbeat Enjoyers said that they returned to work after retirement because they enjoyed working, 78 percent of the female Upbeat Enjoyers gave this reason (see Figures 7–2 and 7–3). Far more Threatened Actives over 65 (63 percent) gave keeping busy as a reason for returning to work as opposed to the Threatened Actives 65 and younger (33 percent).

Females in need, males in business

Far more female Upbeat Enjoyers (73 percent) gave financial need as a reason for returning to work after retirement versus males in this segment (5 percent). In contrast, more male Upbeat Enjoyers (28 percent) and Threatened Actives (23 percent) returned

Figure 7–1   Rate of Retirement and Returning to Work, 65 and Younger and Over 65, 50+ Self Segments

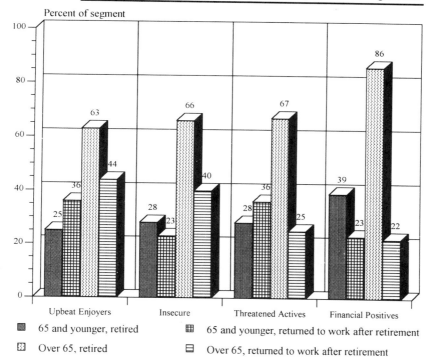

More of those over 65 in all segments have retired, compared to those 65 and younger. However, far more Financial Positives in both age groups have retired. While more Upbeat Enjoyers and Threatened Actives 65 and younger have returned to work since retirement, more over-65 Upbeat Enjoyers have done so.

to work by starting their own businesses as compared to the females in these segments (9 and 0 percent respectively) (see Figures 7–2 and 7–3).

Better planning, rethinking needed

The two most prevalent reasons for returning to work—keeping busy and financial need—point out the insufficiencies that exist in our retirement planning. One key point is that those who returned to work had not intended to do so but, through a lack of planning of one type or another, found that it became necessary.

Employers could encourage the Financial Positives' long-term viewpoint among all their employees. The federal government, for its part, can institute incentives that encourage individual saving for retirement. The fragility of the Social Security system

Figure 7–2   Reasons for Returning to Work, Males, 50+ Self Segments

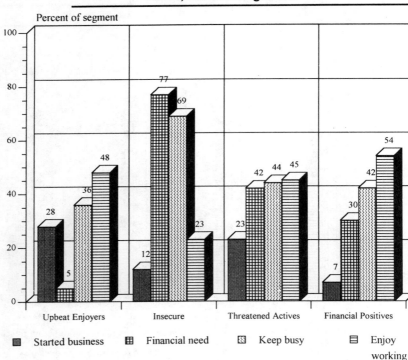

Percent of segment

On a multiple-response question listing five reasons for returning to work after retirement, far more male Insecure found employment due to financial need or to keep busy. More male Financial Positives took a job because they enjoy working, while more male Upbeat Enjoyers started their own businesses.

and its insufficiencies points to the need for more individual responsibility in financing retirement.

Retirement planning, which includes a consideration of activities and financial needs, would structure a secure and more enriching retirement.

Types of jobs

In comparing the types of jobs held previous to retirement to those held after retirement, more of those who had been in professional and technical positions and then retired were able to return to that type of employment. For example, of those Upbeat Enjoyers who had been in professional or technical positions (35 percent) and then retired, more were able to return to such jobs after retirement (31 percent) in contrast to other types of employment.

Figure 7–3   Reasons for Returning to Work, Females, 50+ Self Segments

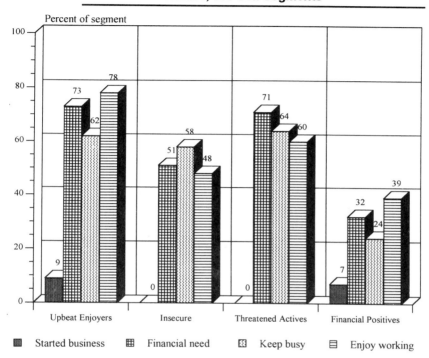

On a multiple-response question listing five reasons for returning to work after retirement, more of both female Upbeat Enjoyers and female Threatened Actives returned due to financial need or to keep busy. In addition, more female Upbeat Enjoyers returned to work because they enjoy working.

More of those over 50 were in clerical jobs after retirement (25 percent) than before (15 percent). The increase is most dramatic among the male Insecure. While 2 percent of those who had retired were in clerical positions before retirement, 53 percent who returned to work were in such positions after retirement.

Scouting the want ads

According to our 50+ study only 4 percent, or 2.5 million, of the over-50 population is currently seeking employment. However, more of those in certain segments and subsegments are searching for jobs.

On one hand, no Financial Positives over 65 are looking for employment. On the other, more female Upbeat Enjoyers (9 percent) are job hunting, as are Insecure 65 and younger (13 percent).

Companies from McDonalds to Kelly Services, Hewlett-Packard to The Travelers, who actively recruit retirees, should benefit from knowing that some Self segments are better targets for their job offers than others. Recruitment advertising, compensation packages, and training should be tailored to attract and retain mature employees in specific segments.

Hours worked per week

Of those over 50 who work, 40 percent continue to work 35 or more hours per week. But far more Upbeat Enjoyers (48 percent) are working these hours than are Financial Positives (38 percent). Even fewer Insecure (32 percent) are working 35 or more hours per week. In fact, 52 percent of the Insecure are not working at all compared to 41 percent of the population over 50.

While almost one in five persons over 50 works part time, or fewer than 35 hours per week, more of the Upbeat Enjoyers (27 percent) work these hours. Far fewer of the remaining three segments work part time. For example, only 16 percent of the Insecure do so.

At the present time, then, more Upbeat Enjoyers, as compared to the other segments, are employed for pay, with 75 percent of them working full or part time.

RETIREMENT PLANNING

Saving begun

Although they have a median age of 64, nearly one in seven of the over-50 population has not yet started saving for retirement on a consistent basis. Of those who have started saving, the median age at which they did so was 44.

The Financial Positives started saving at a median age of 39, the earliest of the four Self segments. In contrast, the Upbeat Enjoyers were 42 years old when they began saving. The Insecure began saving for retirement at the oldest age of the four Self segments: 49. In fact, 23 percent of the Insecure have not yet begun saving.

Saving early for retirement

When examined by gender and age, male Financial Positives began saving for retirement at a median age of 37, earlier than any other subsegment. The female Financial Positives, who began saving for retirement at 41, did so at a younger age than any other female subsegment (see Figure 7–4).

These behaviors coincide with the motivations of the Financial Positives shown in the attitudinal portion of the questionnaire. There, this segment strongly agreed that financial security is something that has to be planned for. They were the only Self segment to agree with this statement.

Written plans on increase

Financial planners should note that only 8 percent of those over 50 live in a household where someone has paid to have a retirement plan written. Virtually the

**Figure 7–4   Median Age at Which Started Saving for
Retirement, Males and Females,
50+ Self Segments**

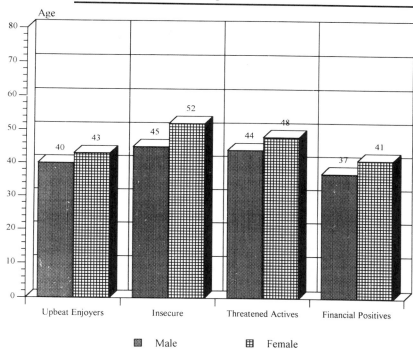

In both the male and female subsegments, the Financial Positives started saving for retirement at a younger age. In contrast, the Insecure began saving at the oldest age in both gender-based subsegments.

same number of Financial Positives, Upbeat Enjoyers, and Threatened Actives (11 to 12 percent) live in such a household.

At least among the Upbeat Enjoyers, Insecure, and Financial Positives, more of those in subsegments 65 and younger than over 65 live in a household where someone has paid to have a retirement plan written. This increase may signal a trend that formal, paid retirement planning is becoming more prevalent.

SOURCES OF FINANCIAL ADVICE

Trusting primarily themselves

Asked to select their one or two primary sources of financial advice from 15 options, 50 percent of the over-50 population relies on itself for such advice. That percentage is highest among the Insecure (56 percent) and Financial Positives (52 percent) (see Figure 7–5).

One's spouse is a top source of financial advice for 18 percent of the population over 50, but for 24 percent of the female Financial Positives. Male Threatened Actives (22 percent) are also going to their spouses for financial advice in numbers higher than the mature population.

Financial planners not widely used

Investors over 50 don't prefer financial planners paid through a commission over those paid by a fee. These types of planners are used by 4 to 5 percent of this population. However, more Upbeat Enjoyers (9 percent) make use of planners paid by commission than do Financial Positives (6 percent). Equal numbers of Upbeat Enjoyers and Financial Positives (6 percent each) make use of fee-based financial planners.

Figure 7–5   Top Three Sources of Financial Advice, 50+ Self Segments

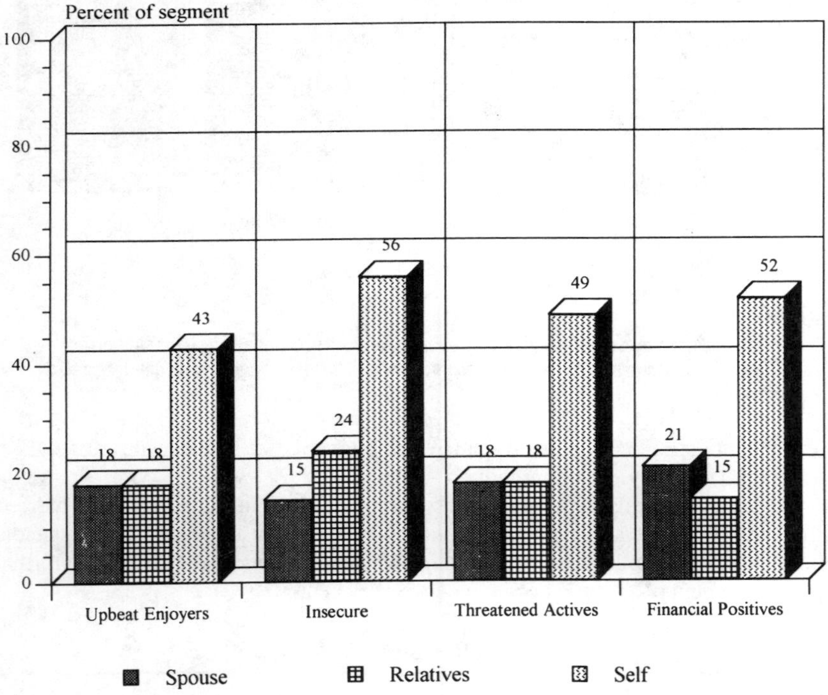

On a question asking for one or two primary sources of financial advice from 15 options, more in all segments rely on themselves, especially the Insecure. In addition, more Insecure rely on relatives for such advice. More Financial Positives rely on their spouses.

Traditional sources outdraw planners

Other, more traditional, sources of advice are attracting more of the Self segments than are financial planners. For example, more Financial Positives (18 percent), especially female Financial Positives (21 percent), go to their stockbroker as compared to the population over 50 (11 percent) (see Figure 7–6).

For 8 percent of the Upbeat Enjoyers, a mutual fund representative serves as a source of financial advice, but he or she serves this function for slightly fewer Financial Positives (6 percent).

Insurance agent relied upon

And at a rate higher than would be expected, more Financial Positives (9 percent) go to their insurance agent for financial advice as compared to those over 50 (7

Figure 7–6   Next Three Sources of Financial Advice, 50+ Self Segments

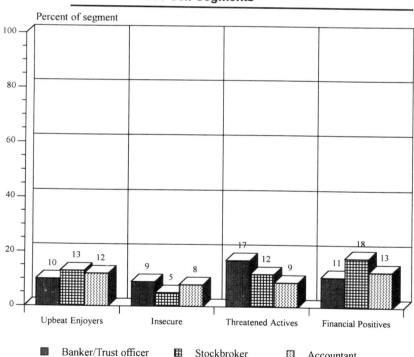

On a question asking for one or two primary sources of financial advice from 15 options, more Threatened Actives rely on a banker or trust officer for financial advice, while more Financial Positives rely on a stockbroker.

percent). Female Financial Positives (11 percent) especially favor their insurance agent for such advice.

Threatened Actives (17 percent) in greater numbers rely on their banker for financial advice as compared to those over 50 (11 percent) (see Figure 7–6). More female Threatened Actives (18 percent) turn to their banker as opposed to male Threatened Actives (16 percent).

Media guides male Upbeat Enjoyers

The media also serve as a source of financial advice for numbers of over-50 consumers. Magazines such as *Money* and *Kiplinger's Personal Finance* are read by far more Financial Positives (14 percent) as compared to persons over 50 (9 percent). But one in five male Upbeat Enjoyers list such magazines as one of their top sources of financial advice.

The same percentages of Upbeat Enjoyers and Financial Positives (4 percent each) watch television programs giving financial advice. But more female Financial Positives (6 percent) are tuning in to programs such as *Wall $treet Week.*

AFFLUENT INVESTORS: KEEPING OPTIONS OPEN

Relying on themselves

We examined the one or two primary sources of financial advice for those in the over-50 population who have investments, excluding their homes, that total $200,000 or more. The investments owned by this affluent group, which represents 19 percent of the mature population, include bonds, stocks, and mutual funds. Affluent investors within each of the Self segments rely on very different sources for financial advice (see Figure 7–7). Whether only affluent mature investors are considered or the entire population over 50, the most frequently cited source of financial advice remains themselves (51 and 50 percent respectively).

Male Upbeat Enjoyers with $200,000 or more in investments rely on themselves (54 percent) and financial magazines (30 percent). In contrast, female Upbeat Enjoyers trust themselves far less (30 percent), but are the segment most likely to go to a financial planner (33 percent). While more affluent female Threatened Actives (59 percent) rely on themselves, their next most relied-upon source of advice is their spouse (45 percent).

Wives a resource

Male Financial Positives with $200,000 or more in investments rely on themselves (53 percent) and their spouses for advice (22 percent). More male Financial Positives seek out their wives for such advice than any other Self segment.

Affluent female Insecure rely on themselves (52 percent), but are also the segment most likely to go to their accountant (47 percent) for financial advice. After themselves (49 percent) and their spouse (18 percent), more affluent female Financial Positives turn to their banker (15 percent) than any other gender-based subsegment.

Relying on stockbroker less

It is true that 32 percent of the affluent mature investors cite their stockbroker as one of their first sources of financial advice. This rate is far higher than that of the population over 50 (11 percent). However, stockbrokers appeal primarily to older affluents in three of the four Self segments. For example, of those over-65 Upbeat Enjoyers with assets of $200,000 plus, 43 percent rely on their stockbroker. In comparison, only 20 percent of affluent Upbeat Enjoyers 65 and younger do so.

More of the affluent Threatened Actives (48 percent) as compared to the other Self segments rely on their stockbroker as a source of financial advice (see Figure 7–7).

Mutual fund rep not a resource

Of the affluent mature investors, only 4 percent rely on a mutual fund representative as their one or two primary sources of financial advice. This rate is about the same as for the population over 50 (5 percent).

Given this insight, one wonders how Fidelity Investments' new strategy of more face-to-face contact with its customers and increased personal guidance will pay off. Regardless of their assets, mutual fund representatives are not thought of by many mature investors as a primary source of financial advice.

WHY AVOID THE PROS?

Products not the problem

Reasons for not going to a professional for financial planning, whether a banker or stockbroker, were addressed in a multiple-choice question with 10 possible responses.

Because marketers often focus solely on product specifications, we must stress that the reasons why those over 50 avoid going to a professional for financial planning are not related to dissatisfaction with the products offered. Only 1 percent of those over 50 avoid professional financial planning because the products aren't good or because the planner doesn't offer a sufficiently wide range of products.

Cost an issue for some

Setting aside any deficiencies in the products themselves, we see that cost is one of the objections which the over-50 population has to going to a professional for financial planning (29 percent). This is an objection for 39 percent of the Insecure but only 18 percent of the Financial Positives (see Figure 7–8).

Trust central to the sale

Cost aside, three reasons for not going to a professional for financial planning focus on the relationship between the client and the planner. They all relate to trust. Based on other research we have conducted, we believe that developing trust is central to the sale of financial products and services.

Although 12 percent of those over 50 say that they avoid professionals for financial planning because they do not trust them, the Threatened Actives (19 percent) more

**Figure 7–7   Top Four Sources of Financial Advice,
Affluent Investors, 50+ Self Segments**

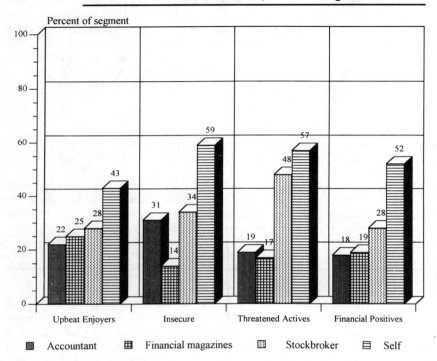

On a question asking for one or two primary sources of financial advice from 15 options, more Insecure who are affluent investors with $200,000 or more in assets excluding their homes rely on accountants or themselves. More affluent Upbeat Enjoyers rely on financial magazines, while more affluent Threatened Actives rely on stockbrokers.

than the other segments embody this distrust (see Figure 7–8). This position parallels the mindset Threatened Actives revealed in the attitudinal portion of the questionnaire. They are a suspicious segment that feel threatened by external forces.

Shearson Lehman's ads stress trust

Many of the television advertisements created by Shearson Lehman Brothers for its 1991 campaign recognize the importance of trust and integrity in the selection of a financial advisor. The advertisements stress the idea of Shearson Lehman as an honest brokerage firm that seeks to establish trusting relationships with clients. One Shearson Lehman commercial in particular explores the personal relationship a 50ish investor has with his financial advisor. The client wants to go to cooking school in

Paris and asks his advisor to align his portfolio so that he can make his dream come true.

Developing trust

Given the importance of trust in the relationship between the mature investor and his or her financial advisor, the advisor must develop specific strategies to foster trust. These strategies could range from more frequent client meetings to additional reports, regular newsletters to occasional seminars.

Confidentiality a concern

A lack of trust is also seen in the fact that almost a quarter of the population over 50 (23 percent) avoids a professional financial advisor because they want to keep their financial affairs private.

In promoting their services to clients, financial professionals should stress confidentiality. These assurances are very important not only to a third of the Threatened Actives, but to some of the other segments as well. For example, even among the Upbeat Enjoyers, one in five avoids financial planners because they want to keep their financial affairs private (see Figure 7–8).

Making more on their own

A third group of reasons for avoiding professionals for financial planning relates to performance. These objections include receiving inferior advice or the fact that some mature investors believe that they can make more money on their own. For example, making more money on their own is something more Financial Positives (25 percent) believe is possible as compared to those over 50 (15 percent).

Of all the subsegments, far more asset-rich male Financial Positives (35 percent) believe they can make more money on their own than by going to a professional for financial planning. More than any other subsegment, this one has the greatest number of investors who rely on their own abilities.

Giving unreliable advice

Other objections related to performance include financial professionals giving unreliable advice and their poor investment performance. Within the mature population, 8 percent believe that financial planners give unreliable advice, but more male Upbeat Enjoyers (18 percent) have this objection. More in this subsegment (14 percent), as contrasted to the population over 50 (6 percent), are also critical of the financial professionals' poor investment performance.

To get business from mature investors, professionals selling financial products and services will have to demonstrate a winning track record for themselves and the products they sell. Understanding the needs and concerns of the Self segments will help financial planners and others to better target their marketing efforts and establish more fruitful relationships.

**Figure 7–8   Reasons for Not Going to a Professional
for Financial Planning, 50+ Self Segments**

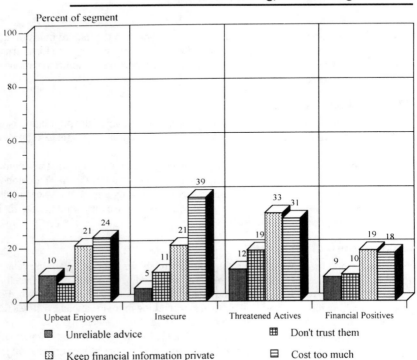

On a multiple-response question listing 11 reasons for not going to professional financial planners,
more Threatened Actives either believe their advice is unreliable, don't trust them, or want to keep
their financial information private. More Insecure feel such services cost too much.

SOURCES OF RETIREMENT SUPPORT

While almost all of the mature population (94 percent) is currently using Social
Security or counting on using it to support retirement, the Financial Positives have
accumulated the most diverse range of resources to support themselves in retirement.
More of them (64 percent), for example, live on a pension now or will do so in the
future as compared to the Insecure (37 percent) and Upbeat Enjoyers (61 percent) (see
Figure 7–9).

Upbeat Enjoyers hard at work

While more Upbeat Enjoyers are still working and are using or will use their current
employment to fund their retirement (25 percent), fewer Financial Positives (15
percent) are doing so (see Figure 7–9). In comparison to the mature population (17

percent), far more male Upbeat Enjoyers (33 percent) now finance or intend to finance their retirement out of current employment.

Pensions differ by gender

Although more males than females in all of the Self segments have a pension, the discrepancy is wider in some of the Self segments than in others. A significant disparity exists between male Threatened Actives (62 percent) and female Threatened Actives (45 percent) on whether or not they receive or will receive a pension.

The difference between male and female pension recipients in the Financial Positive segment is not quite as dramatic. In these subsegments 68 percent of the males receive a pension as compared to 61 percent of the females.

Mutual funds favored

In terms of investments, more of those in two subsegments, female Financial Positives (38 percent) and male Upbeat Enjoyers (36 percent), will rely on mutual funds for retirement income. These percentages are in dramatic contrast to the 23 percent of those over 50 who will finance their retirement with mutual funds.

Bonds are favored by male Financial Positives (22 percent), many more of whom will use them for retirement than the over-50 population (9 percent).

ACCEPTING INVESTMENT RISK

Majority prefer barest minimum risk

The majority of investors over 50 prefer to accept the barest minimal risk (50 percent), but far more Insecure (63 percent) and Threatened Actives (57 percent) feel comfortable with this risk level. This lowest-risk situation is, however, also acceptable to slightly more than a third of the Upbeat Enjoyers and Financial Positives (see Figure 7–10). More female Financial Positives (45 percent) prefer to take the barest minimal risk as compared to male Financial Positives (31 percent).

The Financial Positives, both male and female, have a generally conservative view on investment risk. This position parallels the views toward investment and risk that they revealed in the attitudinal portion of the questionnaire. There they agreed very strongly that "most of my [their] investments are conservative."

Medium risk finds proponents

Substantial numbers of Upbeat Enjoyers (39 percent) and Financial Positives (37 percent) will accept taking a medium risk with a medium rate of return (see Figure 7–10). More than any other subsegment, however, male Upbeat Enjoyers (50 percent) are willing to take this level of risk.

Vast majority avoid high risk

Of the four levels of investment risk that we measured, only an insignificant number of over-50 investors are willing to take a high risk for a potential high return. While only 2 percent of the population over 50 is willing to accept this scenario, 6 percent

**Figure 7–9   Sources of Retirement Support,
50+ Self Segments**

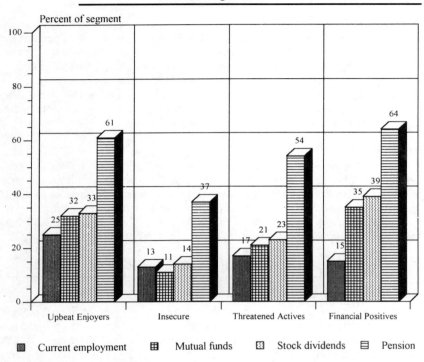

Percent of segment

On a multiple-response question listing 11 sources of financial support for retirement, more Financial Positives rely on pensions compared to the other segments. More Financial Positives also rely on mutual funds and stock dividends as sources of retirement support, while more Upbeat Enjoyers depend on current employment.

of the male Upbeat Enjoyers would. On the other hand, fewer than 1 percent of the Financial Positives would accept this level of risk, which attests to their conservative attitude toward investing (see Figure 7–10).

Affluence increases risk tolerance

Significant differences come to light when we contrast the level of risk tolerated by all mature investors against that of those who are affluent. Although the percentages are still in the single digits, more affluent investors, especially the Upbeat Enjoyers, are willing to assume a high risk in order to achieve a high return. Being affluent does not, however, increase the tolerance of risk among the affluent Financial Positives.

The greatest shift occurs in the tolerance of a medium level of risk for a medium return. Far more affluent investors will tolerate this risk level as compared to mature investors in general. For example, while 39 percent of all Upbeat Enjoyers would tolerate a medium risk, 59 percent of those who are affluent investors will do so (see Figure 7–11).

CONCLUSION

We must use more time, energy, and financial resources in planning for our Third Age. Building the financial underpinnings of a secure retirement is an area in which only one segment, the Financial Positives, has been notably successful.

Retiring and returning to work is a prevalent pattern among two Self segments. Those who seek to employ retirees should analyze these segments' needs in order to improve recruiting. While retirement planning services are needed by those who are now 50, those marketing such services must position them to appeal to specific segments.

Figure 7–10 Preferred Level of Risk, 50+ Self Segments

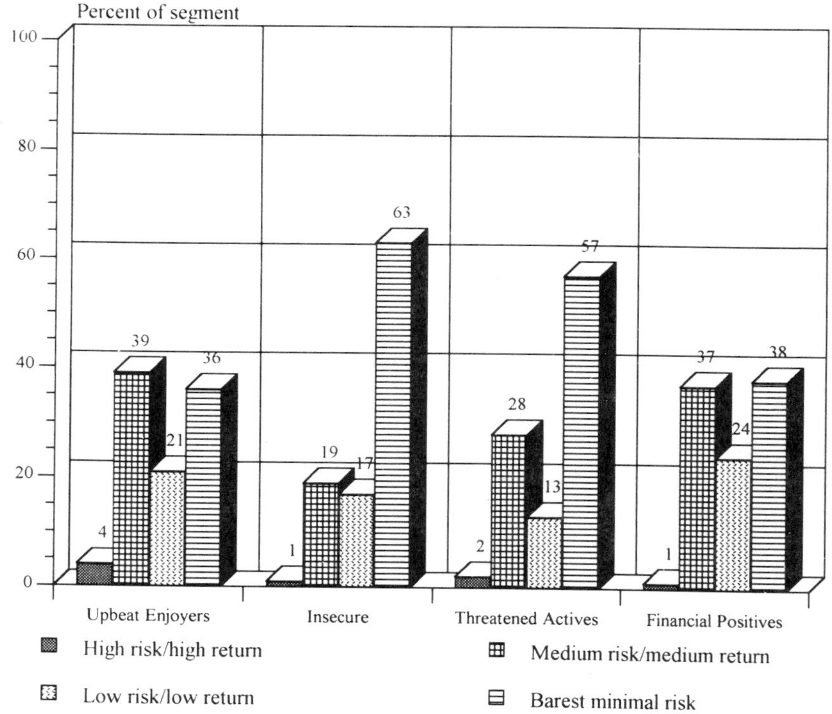

Compared to the other two segments, more Upbeat Enjoyers and Financial Positives are open to taking a medium financial risk with the potential for a medium return. Far more Insecure and Threatened Actives prefer to take the barest minimal risk.

Figure 7–11 Preferred Level of Risk, Affluent Investors, 50+ Self Segments

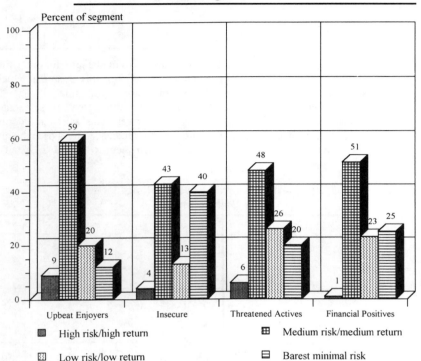

More Upbeat Enjoyers who are affluent investors with assets, excluding their homes, of $200,000 or more, prefer a high or medium financial risk as compared to the other segments. More affluent Threatened Actives prefer a low risk, while more affluent Insecure will take only the barest minimal risk.

Opportunities exist for those who sell financial services and products in dealing with mature investors within the Self segments. Critical to success with these segments, however, is gaining their trust and demonstrating proven success. In addition, knowledge of the Self segments will allow brokers and planners to offer segment-specific investments.

EIGHT

FINANCIAL SERVICES

While she sipped coffee and munched on cookies at her bank's senior club, $50,000 was silently siphoned from her savings account at the bank and into a large, national bond fund. Thoughtfully, she had left $3,000 in her account so that she could still take advantage of the bank's generous offer of free traveler's checks, discounted travel, an accidental death insurance policy, unlimited checking with interest, and discounted eyewear. And cookies, of course.

"Some banks are finding that they really do not understand the needs and wants of the older person," says Michael P. Sullivan, a bank marketing consultant. The lack of understanding that some banks display regarding mature consumers is often related to unfocused and unimaginative marketing.

Banks must devise profitable and innovative services and products they can offer to each of the Self segments within their base of mature customers because, according to Sullivan, mature consumers are their best customers using "three to four times the services of other customers." Without the development of cross-selling skills and competitive products, dollars that mature customers now have on deposit will drift to other institutions and the investments they offer.

This chapter discusses the asset and debt levels of the four Self segments, then goes on to examine specific services that each of the segments currently obtains from its financial institutions. The segments' willingness to purchase innovative services from a bank is also detailed. The chapter concludes with an analysis of each segment's use of specific credit cards.

ASSETS AND LIABILITIES

Amount of money owed

One common stereotype of mature consumers is that they are a group of savers, not borrowers. Admittedly, the debt level of those over 50 is very low. All debts, including a mortgage, for this population total a median of $8,276; 60 percent owe less than $10,000. However, one segment, the Upbeat Enjoyers, makes more use of debt than the rest.

97

In totalling all of their debt, including mortgages, the median amount owed by the four Self segments ranges from $14,079 owed by the Upbeat Enjoyers to $7,351 owed by the Insecure. More Financial Positives (62 percent) and Insecure (68 percent) owe less than $10,000 as compared to the Upbeat Enjoyers (46 percent).

Higher debt level for Upbeat Enjoyers

In contrast, more Upbeat Enjoyers (15 percent) have debts exceeding $100,000 or more as compared to both the population over 50 (8 percent) and the Financial Positives (9 percent). As we will see below, more Upbeat Enjoyers use services from banks that relate to credit and loans than the other Self segments. Opportunities exist for banks to extend credit to the Upbeat Enjoyers, the one Self segment that is both credit worthy and credit prone.

Measuring assets

In considering the assets the Self segments hold, excluding their homes, the Financial Positives ($97,074) have greater assets. The Upbeat Enjoyers are second at $70,617, while the Insecure at $24,130 have the lowest amount in assets.

More Financial Positives (49 percent) have assets above $100,000 as compared to Upbeat Enjoyers (38 percent). In addition, more Financial Positives (11 percent) have assets over $500,000 as compared to Upbeat Enjoyers (7 percent).

Male Financial Positives have highest assets

The subsegment with the highest amount of assets, excluding their homes, is the male Financial Positives, who have a median of $140,300. Male Upbeat Enjoyers are second ($96,729) and the female Financial Positives ($79,585) third.

Those with the lowest level of assets are females in the Insecure ($17,157) and Threatened Active ($20,950) segments. Even their male counterparts have higher assets. Male Insecure, for example, have median assets of $51,898.

RELATIONSHIP WITH FINANCIAL INSTITUTION

Services obtained

In answering a multiple-choice question listing 14 services or products that a mature consumer could obtain from a financial institution such as a bank, savings and loan, or credit union, more Financial Positives use services related to the accumulation, retention, or protection of assets. In contrast, greater numbers of Upbeat Enjoyers use products related to debt.

Use of savings instruments

In the United States, 62 percent of the population has a savings account at a financial institution. If only the population over 50 is considered, however, the number with savings accounts rises to 74 percent. Within the Self segments, savings account ownership rises among the Financial Positives (83 percent), but is only slightly higher than the national norm within the Upbeat Enjoyers (75 percent) (see Figure 8–1).

Seniors own 60 percent of all the dollars in banks. When financial institutions need money for the loans they fund, whether for college or starting new businesses, that money will largely come from the deposits of mature savers.

More Financial Positives hold CDs

Vastly more Financial Positives (55 percent) than Upbeat Enjoyers (36 percent) have a certificate of deposit (CD) (see Figure 8–1). The same percentage of male and female Financial Positives have a CD at a financial institution.

Upbeat Enjoyers better borrowers

More Upbeat Enjoyers (19 percent) than Financial Positives (13 percent) have a car loan at a financial institution. That percentage increases when one considers only Upbeat Enjoyers 65 and younger, 28 percent of whom have a car loan at a financial institution. In comparison, only 5 percent of U.S. adults have a new car loan at a bank.

The role of Upbeat Enjoyers as better borrowers than savers is also seen in the fact that more of them (9 percent) than Financial Positives (5 percent) have a second mortgage.

While 35 percent of male Upbeat Enjoyers have a line of credit, only 23 percent of the male Financial Positives do so. Both of these percentages contrast sharply with the 8 percent of U.S. adults who have a line of credit.

ATM use highest in two segments

In the U.S. population, automatic teller machine (ATM) card penetration has been at 57 percent for the past two years. Of the population over 50, 29 percent have an ATM card. However, the percentages of those who possess an ATM card differ within each of our 50+ segments and their subsegments.

Far more Upbeat Enjoyers and Financial Positives have an ATM card (40 and 38 percent respectively) than the population over 50 (29 percent). In fact, ATM card usage by Upbeat Enjoyers (51 percent) and Financial Positives (49 percent) 65 and younger is far closer to the level of the U.S. population (57 percent).

Fewer ATM cards among two segments

In contrast to the high level of penetration of ATM cards among the Upbeat Enjoyers and Financial Positives, far fewer Insecure (17 percent) and Threatened Actives (29 percent) have ATM cards.

When we examine only those over 65 for the possession of an ATM card, the use of this service drops substantially. For example, 51 percent of the Upbeat Enjoyers 65 and younger have an ATM card, but only 23 percent of those over 65 do. Among the low-usage Insecure, possession of an ATM card falls to the single digits among those over 65 (7 percent).

Making use of plastic

While 30 percent of those in the general U.S. population have a credit card from their bank, credit union, or savings and loan, 55 percent of those over 50 do.

Equal percentages of Upbeat Enjoyers and Financial Positives have a credit card from their financial institution (67 percent each). However, more male Upbeat Enjoyers (75 percent) have a credit card from their financial institution as compared to the other gender-based subsegments.

Getting a credit card through a financial institution is something that fewer Insecure (44 percent) and Threatened Actives (53 percent) do (see Figure 8–1). Among the Self subsegments, fewer Insecure (35 percent) over 65 have a credit card from a financial institution.

Use of debit card low

More recently introduced services such as a debit card are used by 6 percent of the Financial Positives, but by only 3 percent of the population over 50. Today debit card transactions account for only .5 percent of payments to merchants. Although their use is growing, their acceptance by the Self segments remains to be studied.

Keeping things safe

Of all the Self segments, more Financial Positives (53 percent) have a safe deposit box with a financial institution in comparison to the population over 50 (41 percent). In contrast, far fewer Upbeat Enjoyers (40 percent) rent such a box.

INNOVATIVE FINANCIAL SERVICES

Banks as a resource

It is apparent that the Financial Positives feel comfortable receiving a wide variety of services from a financial institution. In asking the Self segments about five less typical services they currently have or would consider obtaining from a bank, savings and loan, or credit union, more Financial Positives than the other segments received such services or would consider receiving them.

These services range from travel arrangements to a stockbrokerage account, property and casualty insurance to financial planning. Clearly, financial institutions should be targeting the Financial Positives and offering them a wide range of fee-based services.

Buying life insurance

At a rate higher than would be expected, far more Financial Positives (34 percent) have life insurance from their financial institution in contrast to those over 50 (25 percent). Another 3 percent of the Financial Positives would consider obtaining life insurance from their financial institution.

In contrast, far fewer Upbeat Enjoyers and Threatened Actives (25 percent each) receive life insurance from their financial institution, although another 4 percent each would consider doing so (see Figure 8–2).

Figure 8–1   Top Four Accounts/Services from a
Financial Institution, 50+ Self Segments

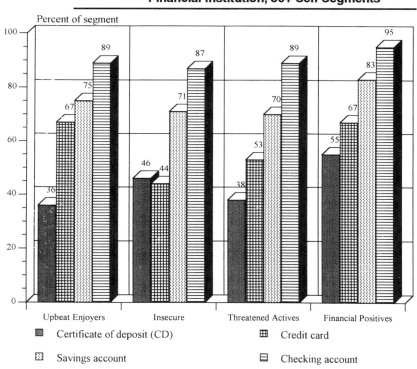

On a multiple-response question listing 14 accounts or services provided by financial institutions, more Financial Positives report currently having certificates of deposit (CDs), savings accounts, and checking accounts.

Buying stocks

As financial institutions become increasingly active in selling stocks and mutual funds, the Financial Positives are the segment to target. For example, 21 percent of the Financial Positives have a stockbrokerage account with a financial institution. In comparison, only 13 percent of the Upbeat Enjoyers have such an account (see Figure 8–2). There are no differences between male and female Financial Positives in their use of such a stockbrokerage account from a financial institution.

Creating a preemptive strategy

Because more high-asset Financial Positives have savings in financial institutions, the danger exists that they will shift their funds into investments at other institutions. Knowing that a substantial portion of Financial Positives view themselves as savvy investors should prompt financial institutions to develop programs and procedures that will retain the Financial Positives—and their assets.

SERVICES FROM A SENIOR CLUB

Is the club concept passé?

The idea of a senior banking club may conjure up images of coffee klatches and tours to local historical sights. Our 50+ study suggests that banks should consider rethinking what their senior club offers, if they have one, and what its offerings should be.

**Figure 8–2   Less Typical Accounts/Services from a
Financial Institution, 50+ Self Segments**

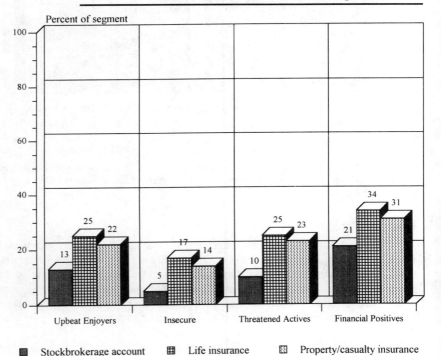

On a multiple-response question listing six less typical accounts or services provided by financial institutions, more Financial Positives report currently having a stockbrokerage account, life insurance, and property/casualty insurance with a financial institution.

Membership limited

Slightly more than a quarter (27 percent) of the over-50 population are members of a senior banking club. However, membership in such a club increases when only those over 65 (35 percent) are considered.

Membership, highest among the Financial Positives (33 percent), rises even more within the over-65 Financial Positives (41 percent). But among Upbeat Enjoyers over 65 (34 percent), membership in a senior banking club is less than the national norm. Clearly, banks are doing a better job of attracting Financial Positives than Upbeat Enjoyers to their senior clubs (see Figure 8–3).

Services most desired

From a list of 14 services, respondents were asked to select five they most desired from a senior club. The top three selected all relate to financial services, not social activities or discounted travel (see Figure 8–4).

Figure 8–3   Membership in a Senior Banking Club, 65 and Younger and Over 65, 50+ Self Segments

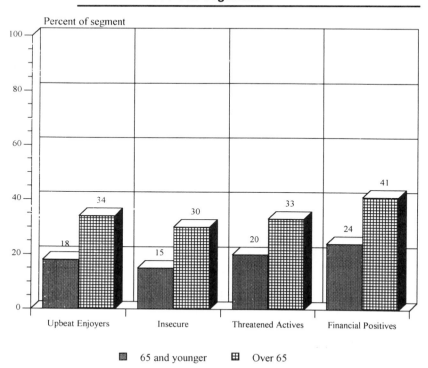

More Financial Positives in both the 65 and younger and over-65 age groups belong to a senior banking club.

One question that could be asked relates to the need for senior banking clubs. If the five most-desired services—from free check printing to a no-fee credit card, free traveler's checks to a free interest-bearing checking account—can be obtained through many packages that banks currently offer to their regular accounts, are senior banking clubs necessary?

Seeking value

The value-driven Financial Positives over 65 are the subsegment most interested in the top five senior club services. For example, although 73 percent of those over 50 want free check printing from a senior club, the service singled out as most important, 80 percent of the Financial Positives over 65 do. In contrast, only 61 percent of Upbeat Enjoyers over 65 want free check printing.

More Financial Positives over 65 than the over-50 population also want the remaining four most desired senior club services, ranging from a Visa card with no annual fee to a free interest-bearing checking account. In addition, more Financial Positives over 65 as compared to Upbeat Enjoyers of that age rate each of these senior club services as important. For example, more Financial Positives over 65 (64 percent) want free traveler's checks, compared to Upbeat Enjoyers over 65 (50 percent).

Social, travel services less appealing

As we have seen, the top five services that the majority of the respondents selected are all financial ones. However, a separate cluster of social or travel-related services attracts one subsegment in particular. Services such as discounts on travel packages, newsletters, special events and activities, and discounts on hotels are of far greater interest to female Financial Positives than they are to the population over 50. On a lesser level, but still higher than the national norm, female Upbeat Enjoyers also desire these socially related services.

Target: Female Financial Positives

For example, more female Financial Positives (33 percent) want discounts on travel packages from their bank's senior club as compared to the population over 50 (19 percent) (see Figure 8–5). Both female Financial Positives and female Upbeat Enjoyers (27 and 26 percent respectively) want discounts on hotels and car rentals, something that only 19 percent of those over 50 are interested in.

MARKETING TO THE SELF SEGMENTS

All too many senior clubs offer me-too services. If financial institutions continue to fund them, senior clubs and the services they offer should provide a competitive advantage in reaching specific Self segments.

Since the offerings currently provided by most senior clubs are more desired by the Financial Positives than by the Upbeat Enjoyers, banks and other financial institutions should consider restructuring their offerings to attract and retain the credit-using Upbeat Enjoyers, as well as the high-asset Financial Positives. For

Figure 8–4   Services Most Desired from a Senior Banking Club, 50+ Self Segments

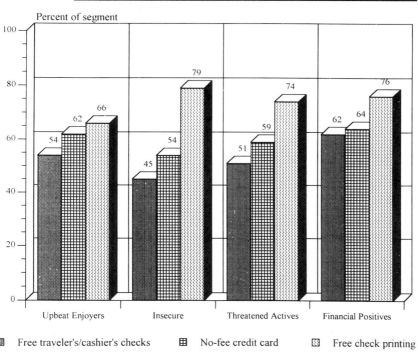

When choosing the five most desired features of a senior banking club from a list of 14, more Financial Positives want free traveler's or cashier's checks and no-fee credit cards. More Insecure want free check printing.

example, if female Financial Positives are currently the most interested in travel-related services from a senior banking club, what other services can be offered to them? They are, after all, a subsegment with $79,585 in assets, excluding their homes.

Financial institutions should adopt a targeted approach to marketing financial services to those in specific Self segments. In doing so they would reposition existing services and create entirely new ones so that value would be added for each of these segments. Ultimately, this strategy would generate more profits for the financial institution.

Building loyalty

As banks and other financial institutions consider the fee-based services they now offer or could offer to those over 50, they must contend with the fact that the majority of mature customers have multiple banking relationships. But besides competition

**Figure 8–5   Social and Travel-Related Services Desired
from a Senior Banking Club,
Males and Females, 50+ Self Segments**

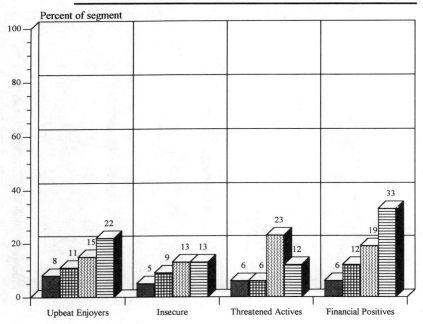

■ Special events, male	⊞ Special events, female	
▨ Discounts on travel packages, male	⊟ Discounts on travel packages, female	

When choosing the five most desired features of a senior banking club from a list of 14 features, far more male Threatened Actives and female Financial Positives want discounts on travel packages. More female Upbeat Enjoyers and Financial Positives want a senior banking club to sponsor special events.

from other financial institutions, firms offering mutual funds and municipal bonds are growing increasingly aggressive and adept at attracting the mature customer's assets.

PATTERNS IN PLASTIC

When asked a multiple-choice question about which of seven types of credit cards they have, more in one segment or another had a preference for a specific card.

Cards carried by Upbeat Enjoyers

More Upbeat Enjoyers carry an American Express card (20 percent) as compared to those over 50 (11 percent) and the Financial Positives (15 percent). Also held by more Upbeat Enjoyers (42 percent) than the population over 50 (32 percent) is a

MasterCard. More Upbeat Enjoyers also have a department store credit card (65 percent) in comparison to the population over 50 (53 percent) (see Figure 8–6).

Financial Positives carry Visa

In contrast, more Financial Positives (60 percent) have a Visa card as compared to Upbeat Enjoyers (54 percent) (see Figure 8–6). In addition, more Financial Positives (15 percent) have an AT&T Visa as compared to the population over 50 (9 percent).

Fewer Insecure possess cards

The wallets of the Insecure contain far fewer credit cards than those of the over-50 population. For example, only 44 percent of the Insecure have a department store credit card compared to 55 percent of those over 50. Only 37 percent of the Insecure have a Visa card in contrast to the population over 50 (47 percent) (see Figure 8–6).

Constellations of cards

Owning only one credit card is not the norm for those over 50, nor for the adult U.S. population. The average American adult has three credit cards. In the 50+ study, those who possess credit cards usually have two or more of them. For example, only 4 percent of the population over 50 has only a Visa card and less than 1 percent has only an American Express card. Of the over-50 population, just 12 percent have only a department store credit card.

Certain combinations of cards are more prevalent than others. Within the mature population, 9 percent of those over 50 have all of the following cards: Diners Club, American Express, MasterCard, Visa, and a department store credit card. At 14 percent, more credit-loving Upbeat Enjoyers have such a combination of cards.

New insights are revealed by studying these card combinations. Having a Visa card, MasterCard, and a department store card is a combination held by 36 percent of the over-50 population and 43 percent of the Financial Positives. In contrast, less than 1 percent of the mature population has only American Express, Diner's Club, and department store credit cards.

Card use revolves around Visa

These various combinations show that for persons over 50, an American Express card functions as an ancillary card. Those over 50 have it in combination with other cards, but not to the exclusion of them. It is much more likely that a Visa card forms the cornerstone of credit card possession by those over 50. Visa, after all, has 144 million cardholders in the U.S. population in comparison to American Express' 25 million cardholders.

Making use of credit cards

Having a credit card, of course, doesn't mean making use of it. A bank credit card is used an average of only 2.3 times a month by those in the U.S. population who have such cards. Those who use a credit card once a week are exceptionally good customers. It's important to note that more of the Upbeat Enjoyers both have and use (26 percent)

**Figure 8–6   Credit Cards Held,
50+ Self Segments**

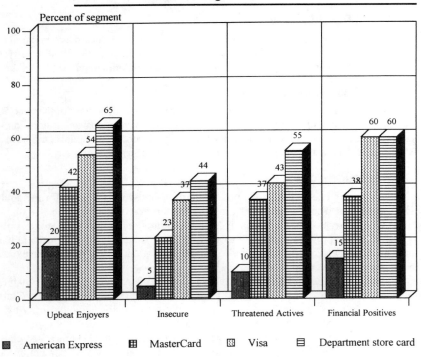

On a multiple-response question on the ownership of eight credit cards, more Upbeat Enjoyers report
having American Express, MasterCard, and a department store card.

an American Express card at least once a week as compared to Financial Positives (17
percent). Even higher use of the American Express card is seen among the male Upbeat
Enjoyers, fully a third of whom are using this card at least once a week.

The idea of a specific Self segment having a credit card and not using it is also
illustrated by the Visa card. Although more Financial Positives (60 percent) than
Upbeat Enjoyers (54 percent) have a Visa card, almost equal percentages of them use
it once a week or more (28 and 29 percent respectively).

More male Upbeat Enjoyers (68 percent) and female Financial Positives (65
percent) have a Visa card. However, more male Upbeat Enjoyers and male Financial
Positives (34 percent each) use their Visa cards once a week or more as compared to
female Financial Positives (26 percent).

Nonuse of cards

Between 7 and 29 percent of those over 50 who hold credit cards never use them. This rate of nonusage is lowest among such cards as American Express (8 percent) and MasterCard (7 percent). A substantial percentage of those over 50 who have a Discover Card never use it (18 percent). Nonuse is highest among those who have a Diner's Club card (29 percent).

Paying up

When it comes to making payments on credit card purchases, 97 percent of those over 50 pay off their American Express card each month. This corresponds to the terms under which this card is issued.

Approximately two-thirds of those over 50 pay off their credit card debt each month on those cards that charge interest. More than the other Self segments, the Financial Positives typically pay the entire balance off each month on these cards. For example, in the case of Visa, far more Financial Positives (74 percent) pay off their balance in full each month as compared to the Upbeat Enjoyers (60 percent) and Insecure (66 percent).

Compared to the Financial Positives, greater numbers of Upbeat Enjoyers and Threatened Actives pay more than the minimum payment, but less than the full balance on their credit card debt. For example, more Threatened Actives (49 percent) and Upbeat Enjoyers (40 percent) pay either the minimum payment or more on their Visa card. In contrast, only 26 percent of the Financial Positives do so.

Upbeat Enjoyers best credit card target

The way in which they pay off their credit-card balances is only one indication of the fact that the Upbeat Enjoyers rely on credit to maintain their lifestyle. The fact that they combine the second highest household income and level of assets with a reliance on credit makes the Upbeat Enjoyers the best over-50 target for credit card companies.

CONCLUSION

Those banks that have taken the mature population for granted can no longer afford to do so. Marketers at financial institutions should critically examine the products and services that they offer to those over 50. Some should be repositioned, others may be discarded.

As competition continues to intensify for every investment dollar, programs must be put into place that capture the mature investor's dollars before they leave the bank, savings and loan, or credit union. Entirely new fee-based services offered to specific Self segments can become important sources of revenue.

Those who issue credit cards should consider the Upbeat Enjoyers as the best target for their services. In addition, credit card companies can study the needs of Upbeat Enjoyers to sell them the additional products and services that they value. These services could include those related to travel, art, or automobiles.

REFERENCES

Advertisement for Visa, *Business Week,* January 11, 1993, p. 25.

"Credit Cards—Holders, Numbers, Spending, and Debt, 1980 and 1989, and Projections, 2000," *Statistical Abstract of the United States 1991,* Table 832, p. 510.

"Fast Facts," *Mature Market Report,* September 1988, p. 5.

"Household Net Worth—Ownership, Median Value of Asset Holdings, and Distribution of Net Worth, by Asset Type: 1984 and 1988," *Statistical Abstract of the United States 1991,* Table 759, p. 468.

"Quick Takes," *Public Relations Journal,* December 1989, p. 11.

Saporito, Bill, "Who's Winning the Credit Card War?" *Fortune,* July 2, 1990, pp. 66-71.

"Seniors Are Prime ATM Target," *American Banker,* December 9, 1991, p. 8A-9A.

Sullivan, Michael P., "Mature Marketing to Mature Americans," *Bankers Monthly,* July 1991, p. 36.

"Who Uses Banking Services?" Report on findings from the Survey of American Consumers by Mediamark Research, Inc., *Quirk's Marketing Research Review,* November 1990, p. 18.

NINE

DEALING WITH CHANGE

LIFE IS CHANGE

"How did this happen?" the woman wonders as she peers into the mirror. Instead of the smooth-skinned, auburn-haired girl she thinks she is, the reflection she confronts is that of another woman, this one with gray hair and wrinkles. Time has marched relentlessly on, and change has inevitably occurred.

Our 50+ study establishes that each Self segment reacts to change, whether in the form of new, innovative products or the aging process, in very different ways. The attitudinal portion of the questionnaire reflects the Self segments' positions toward change. For example, the Upbeat Enjoyers enthusiastically embrace the idea that being open to change is important to a higher quality of life, while the Threatened Actives reject this concept.

How those over 50 deal with change—whether in the realm of new, high-tech products or regarding their own features—is the focus of this chapter. We begin by considering receptivity to innovations in electronics and other products. Resistance to change regarding one's place of residence is examined. How various Self segments adapt to the process of aging is also analyzed. When do the segments consider someone as being "old"? Finally, we look at indications of how each of the Self segments deals with some of the issues surrounding death.

ACCEPTING TECHNOLOGY

Some mature consumers progressive

Although many marketers have dismissed consumers over 50 as unreceptive to high-tech products and services, our research indicates that such a sweeping generalization is not accurate. Some mature consumers are very interested in innovative products, others far less so.

One demonstration of the acceptance of new technologies by those over 50 is the microwave oven. While 75 to 80 percent of all U.S. households have a microwave, 83 percent of those over 50 do. However, at a rate higher than would be expected,

111

more Financial Positives (89 percent) have this appliance. As we show below, male Financial Positives, and often their female counterparts, are consistently the segment most interested in innovative electronic products.

MARKETABLE PHONE-BASED SERVICES

In considering seven services that could be offered by a telecommunications company, only one emerged as having wide appeal. While one of the six remaining services was of very little interest, the other five services appealed to only about one-third of the over-50 population.

It is important to note that in the case of all seven services, male Financial Positives showed levels of interest that were consistently far higher than that of the other subsegments and of the population over 50.

Seeing caller's number

The service that 60 percent of the over-50 population would definitely or probably be interested in is being able to see a display on one's own telephone of the phone number of the person calling. While this concept won the highest level of interest of all seven services, it was particularly popular with male Financial Positives (73 percent) (see Figure 9–1) and the Insecure 65 and younger (71 percent). The number of Upbeat Enjoyers interested in this concept only matches the national norm.

Some services won't win

The high-tech idea that was of least interest was that of using the telephone to log in on a doctor's computer to record when medicine had been taken. Of the mature population, only 14 percent said that they definitely or probably would be interested in such a service. Most interested in this service are the male Financial Positives (22 percent) and Upbeat Enjoyers (22 percent) 65 and younger.

EFT finds adherents

About one in three of the mature population said that it was definitely or probably interested in the remaining five communications-based services, including electronic funds transfer (EFT). While 29 percent of the over-50 population definitely would be interested in EFT, three subsegments show even greater interest.

The subsegments most interested in EFT are the male and female Financial Positives (37 and 34 percent respectively) and male Upbeat Enjoyers (34 percent) (see Figure 9–2). The 50+ study measured interest, not usage. Some of those expressing interest may currently be using EFT.

Although not totally comparable, these levels of interest are higher than those expressed in a survey conducted by the National Automated Clearing House Association. In that survey, 12 percent of those who did not now use EFT expressed interest in using it. The large percentage of Upbeat Enjoyers and Financial Positives who are interested in EFT is further proof that some of those over 50 are receptive to new technology.

As we saw in Chapter 8 on financial services, the Upbeat Enjoyers and Financial Positives possess ATM cards at a level which approaches that of the population as a whole. When these two segments are averaged in with the low-receptivity Insecure and Threatened Actives, however, a distorted picture emerges. This average view understates the acceptance of high-tech products and services by certain Self segments.

Products interest male Financial Positives

One currently available, although expensive, product, the video phone, is of interest to 37 percent of those over 50, but to 52 percent of the male Financial Positives (see Figure 9–2). This subsegment is also most interested in the idea of a "portable" phone number one could use when moving around the country (see Figure 9–1).

Receiving cable television programs via a phone line rather than through a cable company is a service in which more male Financial Positives (49 percent) than those in the over-50 population (32 percent) would definitely or probably be interested.

Figure 9–1   Interest in Electronic Innovation, Males and Females, 50+ Self Segments

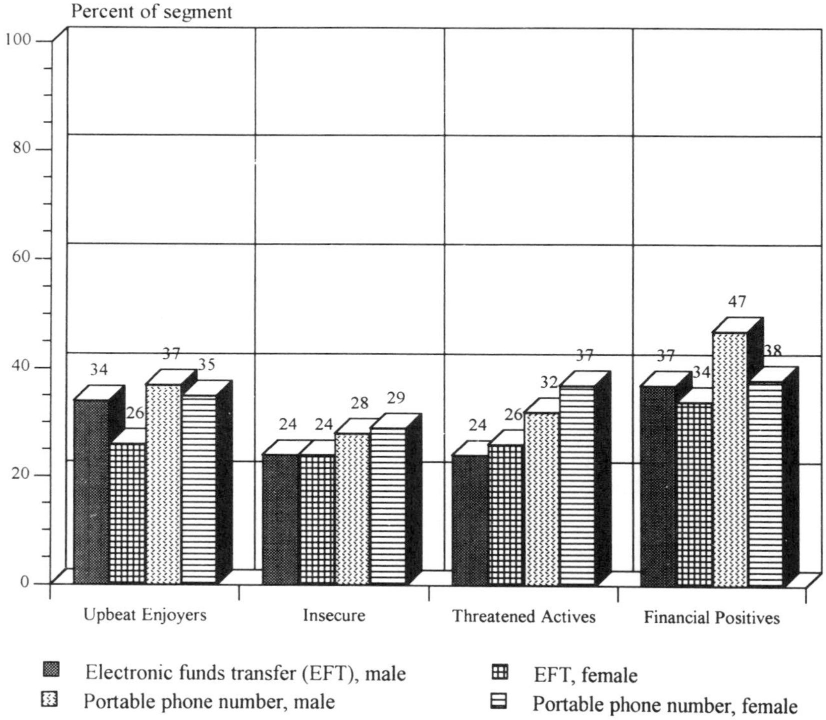

On a multiple-response question listing seven new telephone technologies, more male and female Financial Positives indicate an interest in electronic funds transfer and a portable phone number.

Computers popular with Upbeat Enjoyers

In contrast to the passive telecommunications products that interest the male Financial Positives, computers, which demand a large personal investment, are of greater interest to Upbeat Enjoyers. As compared to the population of those over 50 (11 percent), data from our 1989 50+ study shows that more Upbeat Enjoyers (25 percent) currently use a personal computer. Use is highest among female Upbeat Enjoyers (29 percent) as compared to males (20 percent).

While more than twice as many Upbeat Enjoyers (21 percent) as compared to the population over 50 (9 percent) already own a computer, those in this segment are also the most interested in purchasing a personal computer. For example, while only 18 percent of the mature population is either highly or somewhat interested in purchasing a personal computer, 30 percent of the Upbeat Enjoyers are.

**Figure 9–2   Interest in Electronic Innovation,
Males and Females, 50+ Self Segments**

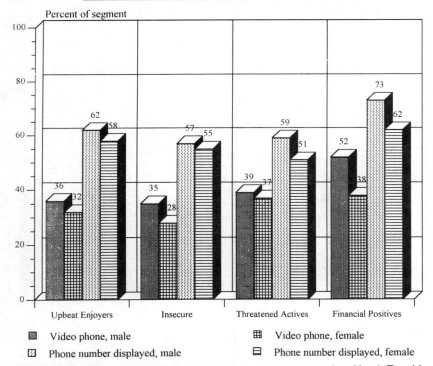

On a multiple-response question listing seven new telephone technologies, more male and female Financial Positives indicate an interest in video phone and a display showing the number of the person calling.

MARKETING TECHNOLOGY TO THE MATURE

Source of feedback

Marketers of leading-edge products and services would find male Financial Positives a highly useful source of feedback. However, this subsegment, ahead of the others in its interest in and receptivity toward technology, should not be taken as representative of those over 50. One or two male Financial Positives who happen to be in a focus group would give high-tech marketers a very misleading picture of the mature consumers' interest in an innovative product.

Marketing high-tech products

Advanced products must also relate to each segment's needs. In terms of their attitudes, Financial Positives have some fear of being victims of a crime. A product that the male Financial Positives might be interested in is Honeywell's TotalHome, a home automation system. This product combines heating and air-conditioning control with security. Besides a user-friendly remote-control device, TotalHome also includes fixed emergency buttons that can be situated throughout the home. While one-quarter of the market for alarms and smoke detectors is made up of U.S. households over 55, vastly more male Financial Positives could be interested in TotalHome.

HOUSING OPTIONS: STAYING PUT

Although one prevalent misconception about retirees is that they have all gathered in Sun City, Arizona, abandoning their past lives and former homes, the truth is far from that. Of those over 60, 83 percent say that they never want to move. In a 1986 AARP study, 46 percent of all respondents over 60 had lived in their current residence for 20 years or more. In addition, Bernard Cohen of the University of Pittsburgh, in studying the records of people who have died, estimates that "average Americans spend about 70 percent of their lives in their final area of residence."

In the attitudinal portion of our questionnaire, three of the four Self segments agreed that they would be happy if they could "live the rest of their lives in their own homes." One segment, the Upbeat Enjoyers, did not find this concept appealing. As we will see below, this segment lives more frequently in condominiums and retirement communities.

Because staying in their own homes is so important to those over 50, other housing options have slight appeal. Holding on to the idea of staying in their homes, more than half of mature Americans have given little thought to their future housing needs.

Renting versus owning

One reason why those over 50 resist moving to another residence is because, most typically, they own the place where they live (80 percent), whether it is a condominium or a single, detached home. Of the houses owned and lived in by those over 65, 83 percent are owned free and clear.

For many homeowners over 50, particularly in segments such as the Insecure, a house or condominium represents both a repository of memories and a significant portion of their assets. But, as we will see below in a section on reverse mortgages, few mature adults have tapped into their home's equity.

More Financial Positives own homes

Of all the Self segments, the Financial Positives (89 percent) are far more likely to own their dwelling. Those Financial Positives 65 and younger (95 percent) are the subsegment most likely to own the place in which they live.

Renting less prevalent

The rental option is chosen by 16 percent of those over 50, but by far more Insecure (25 percent). The percentage who rent increases even further among the Upbeat Enjoyers (29 percent) and Insecure over 65 (28 percent). Examined by gender, male Insecure (28 percent) are most likely to rent.

Living in a house

While 77 percent of those over 50 live in a house, more of the Threatened Actives (82 percent) and Financial Positives (81 percent) do. Although they have very different incomes and levels of assets, these segments agree more strongly than the Insecure that they would be "really happy if they could live the rest of their lives in their own home."

For all the Self segments, fewer of those over 65 live in a house as compared to those 65 and younger. This drop is most dramatic with the Upbeat Enjoyers. More of those 65 and younger (84 percent) live in a house as compared to those over 65 (66 percent). As we will see below, a substantial portion of those Upbeat Enjoyers over 65 who move out of their homes take up residence in apartments.

Insecure are apartment dwellers

While fewer of the Insecure live in a house, far more live in an apartment (21 percent) than does the over-50 population (12 percent) or any other Self segment. On the other hand, fewer Threatened Actives (7 percent) and Financial Positives (9 percent) live in apartments.

Apartment living increases with age

As perhaps a concession to aging, apartment living does increase among all the Self subsegments over 65. While 5 percent of the Upbeat Enjoyers 65 and younger live in an apartment, of those over 65, 17 percent live in this type of dwelling. Far more than the other Self segments, however, the Insecure are primarily apartment dwellers, regardless of age. While 13 percent of the Insecure 65 and younger live in an apartment, 27 percent of those over 65 do so.

The condo option

Living in a condominium, townhouse, or duplex appeals to more of the Upbeat Enjoyers (9 percent) than to those in the over-50 population (5 percent). This behavior corresponds with the fact that in the attitudinal portion of the questionnaire, the Upbeat Enjoyers were the only Self segment to agree that "living in a condominium really appeals to me."

Although 5 percent of those over 50 can be found living in a condominium, townhouse, or duplex, that level drops to 4 percent when only those over 65 are considered. The decrease is concentrated within the Threatened Active and Financial Positive segments.

Living in a mobile home

While a mobile home houses 4 percent of the mature population, it shelters more female Insecure, male Threatened Actives, and Threatened Actives over 65 (7 percent each).

Allure of retirement community

Considering the great enthusiasm that three of the four Self segments have about continuing to live in their own homes, it's not surprising that only 1 percent of the over-50 population lives in a retirement community. Overall, the two segments most open to the retirement home concept are the Upbeat Enjoyers and the Insecure. Among the Upbeat Enjoyers over 65, living in a retirement community increases to 4 percent.

Living with children

The 1989 50+ study shows that only 6 percent of the over-50 population lives with their grown children. More of the Upbeat Enjoyers and Financial Positives (17 percent each) over 65 live with their children. In contrast, fewer Insecure and Threatened Actives (6 and 7 percent respectively) over 65 live with their grown children.

Examined by gender, living with children is more prevalent among females as opposed to males in every Self segment. For example, more female Upbeat Enjoyers (17 percent) live with their grown children than their male counterparts (8 percent).

Maintaining two residences

The flexibility to move between two residences is enjoyed by one in ten of the population over 50. Of the Financial Positives, 12 percent live at a residence other than their primary one for more than three months out of the year, slightly more than the Upbeat Enjoyers (11 percent).

Moving in near future

According to a study by the National Association of Realtors, 75 percent of homeowners said they expected to move at least once during the next ten years. However, a study completed by the National Association of Home Builders shows that, in reality, half of all homeowners are in the same home ten years after purchase, and more than half of that group will still be in the same house after 30 years.

In 1990, about one in five of the U.S. population over a year old actually did move. Of those over 50, one in seven anticipates moving within the next three years. However, much of the mature population's potential movement is concentrated in two segments: male Upbeat Enjoyers (24 percent) and Upbeat Enjoyers 65 and younger (20 percent) (see Figure 9–3).

Reverse mortgage: still rare

No one in our 1991-92 study had a reverse mortgage from their financial institution. This situation can be explained by the fact that, to date, only 152,000 reverse mortgages have been written. Fewer than 1 percent of the over-50 population has a reverse mortgage. Many mature persons are also apparently confused about the term *reverse mortgage.*

Figure 9–3   Anticipate Moving, Males and Females, 65 and Younger and Over 65, 50+ Self Segments

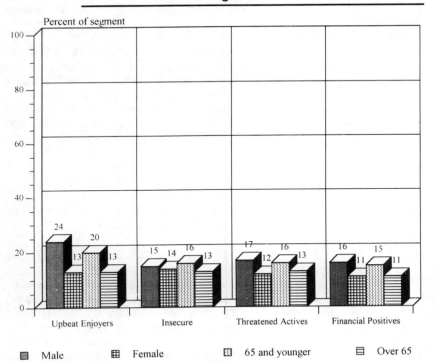

Compared to all other gender- and age-based subsegments, far more male and 65 and younger Upbeat Enjoyers anticipate moving within the next three years.

AGE AS A CONCEPT

What age is old?

While twenty-five years ago those over 50 probably considered someone 65 as old, the median age at which today's mature population considers someone to be old is 84. There are some slight, but interesting, variations between the Self segments on this question. For example, the downtrodden Insecure consider 82 old; the energetic and successful Upbeat Enjoyers think of 85 as old. For all of the subsegments based on age, old is somewhere between 82 and 85. For the Upbeat Enjoyers over 65, however, old has been pushed out to a median of 87 years of age.

What you call them

Having arrived at the Third Age, those over 50 find themselves addressed or described in terms and phrases denoting their age and calling attention to this change.

There has been much discussion about what to call those over 50. In responding to a list of seven options from which they were to select one, one in five respondents to our 1989 50+ study said they preferred no reference to age, suggesting that growing older either be ignored or be deemed irrelevant.

Overall, the term most often cited as the one preferred was *seniors* (23 percent). But since this term was selected by less than a majority of those over 50 and each Self segment showed its own preferences, we conclude that no one term or phrase will satisfy all of the Self segments. For example, while *senior* was the preferred selection of more Insecure (40 percent), it was selected by far fewer Upbeat Enjoyers (9 percent). While using no reference to age was preferred by 27 percent of the Upbeat Enjoyers, it was selected by only 14 percent of the Insecure.

Referring to someone over 50 as a *retiree* was preferred by one in five Threatened Actives and Financial Positives; fewer Upbeat Enjoyers (8 percent) and Insecure (6 percent) found it acceptable.

No universal phrase

Given the fact that no single term is preferred by all the Self segments, it's not surprising that those writing advertising copy are confused about what to call mature consumers. Marketers targeting a specific Self segment should use the term which that segment prefers.

AURA OF YOUTH

Attitudes determine cosmetics use

In the attitudinal portion of the questionnaire, the Financial Positives reveal their belief that their financial planning has enabled them to attain economic sufficiency. While the Financial Positives are satisfied with their bank accounts, they are less happy about the changes that have taken place in their physical appearance.

Attractiveness lessened with age

For example, the Financial Positives don't feel much younger than before, sexier than ever, or more attractive with age. However, they consider it important to "look as young as possible" in a culture that they don't believe places too much emphasis on youth.

Perceiving that their physical attractiveness has diminished, the Financial Positives rely far more than the other Self segments on cosmetics to achieve the illusion of youth. From mascara to lipstick, makeup to eye cream, far more female Financial Positives use every type of cosmetic or treatment product as compared to females in the other Self segments.

The Insecure, whose attitudes generally parallel the Financial Positives regarding their decreased physical attractiveness, also express similar interest in treatment products. The female Insecure are right behind the female Financial Positives in terms of the number of them using cosmetics and treatments.

Upbeat Enjoyers look great naturally

On the other hand, fewer Upbeat Enjoyers, who told us in the attitudinal portion of the questionnaire that they feel much younger than they really are and "sexier than ever," make use of cosmetics than the female Financial Positives.

Financial Positives combat wrinkles

Interested in products that will make their skin look younger, more female Financial Positives than the other female subsegments make regular use of moisturizers and face creams. Female Financial Positives (72 percent) in far greater numbers regularly use moisturizers compared to female Upbeat Enjoyers (54 percent).

Night creams are regularly used by more female Financial Positives (34 percent) as compared to the female Upbeat Enjoyers (21 percent) (see Figure 9–4). In addition, while only 7 percent of the female Threatened Actives use eye cream, 17 percent of the female Financial Positives do.

Of all the Self subsegments, the female Financial Positives ($21.61) spend more every four weeks on personal grooming items than the over-50 population ($14.91). Getting to know this subsegment, overconsumers of treatment products and cosmetics, is important to marketers of Oil of Olay, as well as to Elizabeth Arden.

While those over 55 will account for almost a third of the forecasted $2.1 billion that will be spent on facial care products in 1993, a disproportionate number of those dollars will be spent by female Financial Positives.

Cosmetics a must for Financial Positives

The illusion of youth, or at least of good health and conventional attractiveness, can be created by the artful use of cosmetics. More female Financial Positives, all committed to looking as youthful as possible, are overusers of every type of cosmetic.

Compared to 51 percent of the female Threatened Actives, 74 percent of the female Financial Positives regularly use makeup (see Figure 9–4). In addition, 90 percent of the female Financial Positives use lipstick and 48 percent use mascara. Their level of usage contrasts to that of the female Threatened Actives, of whom only 64 percent use lipstick and 32 percent use mascara regularly. It's clear that far more female Financial Positives regularly present themselves to the world in full makeup.

Covering gray hair

Gray hair, a sure sign of aging, is dyed on a regular basis by 26 percent of the females and 5 percent of the males over 50. More female Financial Positives (31 percent) dye their hair than female Upbeat Enjoyers (23 percent). Among male subsegments, more male Financial Positives (9 percent) dye their hair.

TAKING CARE OF FINAL BUSINESS

Living wills

Coming to terms with one's mortality and the approach of death can include writing a living will. Of the population over 50, 29 percent have made a living will. More of the Financial Positives have written up such an instrument (38 percent), and even more of those in this segment over 65 (47 percent) have done so (see Figure 9-5). Considering the proclivity to plan that the forward-thinking Financial Positives have displayed in other areas of their lives, this high percentage should come as no surprise.

Right to die

Respondents were asked to consider a multiple-choice question presenting five conditions under which they would accept actions that would *allow the death* of a terminally ill patient. The majority of those over 50 agree that the advice of a doctor (51 percent), the patient's request (53 percent), and the existence of a living will (58 percent) would be three acceptable conditions.

Within the Self segments there are differences regarding the acceptability of these three reasons. A doctor's advice to allow the death is acceptable as a reason to more Financial Positives (55 percent) as compared to Upbeat Enjoyers (48 percent). Female Financial Positives (59 percent) in particular accept this as a circumstance, but far fewer female Upbeat Enjoyers (44 percent) do so.

A patient's request to be allowed to die has more weight for the Insecure (59 percent), particularly for the male Insecure (65 percent), as compared to the over-50 population (53 percent).

Examined by age-based subsegments, in every segment far more of those 65 and younger would accept the request of a patient to be allowed to die as compared to those over 65. For example, whereas 64 percent of the Financial Positives 65 and younger would accept the patient's request, only 44 percent of those over 65 would do so.

Finally, far more Financial Positives (64 percent) than Threatened Actives (46 percent) would accept the existence of a living will as a circumstance under which death of a terminally ill patient would be allowed. More than any other subsegment, female Financial Positives (68 percent) would accept the dictates of a living will and allow such a patient to die.

**Figure 9–4   Cosmetics Used,
Females, 50+ Self Segments**

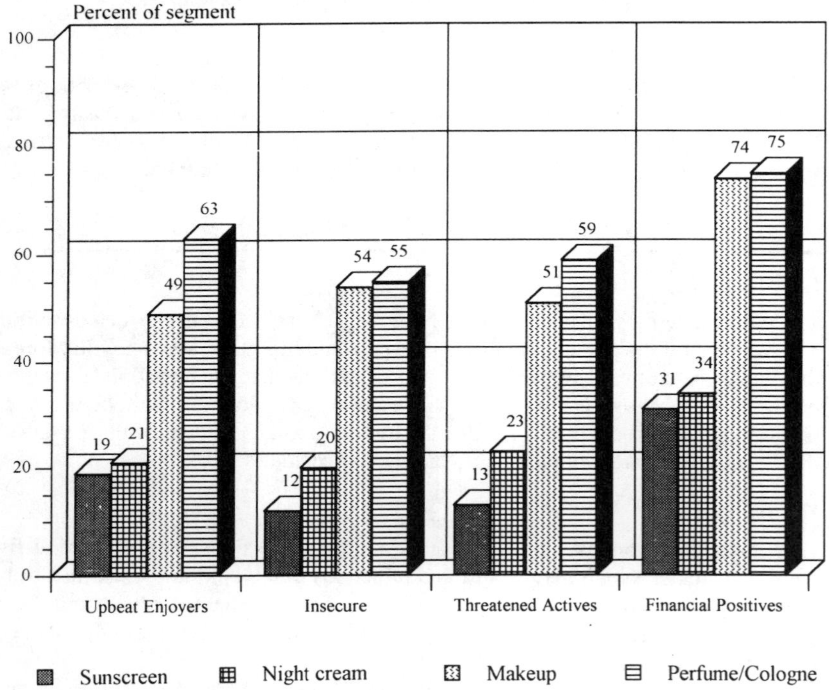

Percent of segment

| | Sunscreen | Night cream | Makeup | Perfume/Cologne |

On a multiple-response question on the use of 16 cosmetics and haircare products, far more female Financial Positives report regularly using sunscreen, night cream, makeup, and perfume or cologne.

Family less influential

The family's request that a terminally ill patient be allowed to die is a circumstance acceptable to only 32 percent of the population over 50. It was least acceptable to the Threatened Actives (30 percent) and most acceptable to the Upbeat Enjoyers (34 percent). Among the subsegments, more male Insecure (42 percent) believe that a family's request to allow a terminally ill patient to die should be honored.

Interestingly, in the age-based subsegments, more of those in every subsegment 65 and younger would allow such a request as compared to those over 65. While 38 percent of the Threatened Actives 65 and younger would honor a family's request, only 22 percent of those over 65 would do so.

This drop in acceptance by age parallels that which we saw above regarding the patient's request that he or she be allowed to die. Are those over 65 more mistrustful

Figure 9–5   Living Wills, Males and Females,
65 and Younger and Over 65,
50+ Self Segments

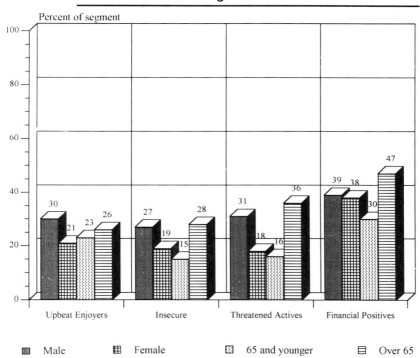

Male ▦   Female ⊞   65 and younger ⊠   Over 65 ⊟

Far more Financial Positives in all gender- and age-based subsegments have living wills.

of both the patient's and family's request that death be allowed to occur as compared to those 65 and younger?

The idea that allowing a terminally ill patient to die is not acceptable under any circumstance finds adherents in slightly more than one out of ten in the U.S. population over 50 (12 percent). Fewer Financial Positives (8 percent) agree with this position, but more Upbeat Enjoyers and Threatened Actives (14 percent each) do so. More female Upbeat Enjoyers (18 percent) in particular would not allow such a death to take place under any circumstances.

Thinking about death and dying

The vast majority (91 percent) of those over 50 think about death and dying. More of the Financial Positives (94 percent) do so as compared to Threatened Actives (86 percent). Having such thoughts rarely or sometimes is something that occurs for more

Financial Positives (85 percent) as compared to those over 50 (79 percent). In contrast, slightly more Insecure and Threatened Actives (12 percent each) think about death and dying frequently or always, as compared to the mature population (11 percent).

Examined by subsegment, 17 percent of the female Threatened Actives have thoughts about death and dying frequently or always, as compared to the over-50 population (11 percent) and to male Threatened Actives (8 percent). In every gender-based subsegment, more females than males have thoughts about death and dying frequently or always.

The suicide option

The rate of suicide for those over 65 is substantially higher than that for the general population. The National Center for Health Statistics reports that 12 suicides occur for every 100,000 people in the total population. However, 17 suicides take place among those over 65. The suicide rate per 100,000 white males aged 65 to 74 is 38. This rate is seven times that for older white women.

Who considers suicide

In the 50+ study, more of those in the Insecure segment consider suicide than in the others. In terms of both attitudes and demographics, the Insecure fit the profile of the older person most apt to commit suicide. We have described the Insecure as lonely, concerned about financial survival, and feeling unlucky and unsuccessful. More Insecure (18 percent) than those over 50 (12 percent) agree with the statement that they have felt so overwhelmed by life that they have considered suicide. Even more male Insecure (21 percent) than female (16 percent) consider suicide (see Figure 9–6).

While less than 1 percent of the over-50 population considers suicide frequently or always, another 11 percent considers it rarely or sometimes. Overall, the Upbeat Enjoyers and Financial Positive segments consider suicide at rates lower than the national norm.

CONCLUSION

Marketers of innovative products should not dismiss the mature customer as uninterested because of age. Clearly, the affluent male Financial Positives should be considered as a potential niche market that is highly receptive to certain technologies.

Most of those over 50 own mortgage-free homes and would like to stay in them. Those who run retirement communities must be highly sophisticated target marketers to reach those who are not only interested in such a living arrangement, but financially able to afford it.

Our problem in agreeing on an acceptable word or phrase that names those who are older reflects this group's own desire not to be considered as old. A phrase such as the Third Age, used in Europe and South America, does not carry the stigma of "retiree" or "senior."

For the Upbeat Enjoyers, aging and the loss of youth means far less than to the Financial Positives. The former segment considers itself to be sexier than ever and

Figure 9–6   Considered Suicide,
Males and Females, 50+ Self Segments

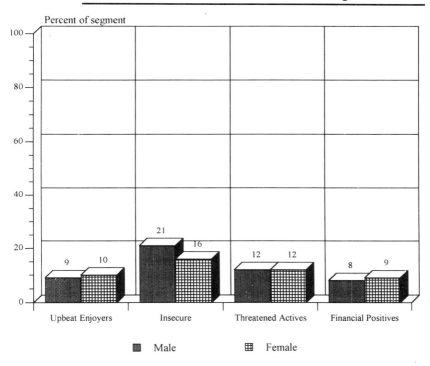

Compared to all other gender-based subsegments, more Insecure, male or female, have been so overwhelmed by life that they have considered suicide.

vital; the latter, regardless of how financially secure, wants to look as young as possible. The Financial Positives' desire to look young and their overconsumption of every type of treatment and cosmetic are very important to marketers of such products. The Financial Positives have not shown themselves to be the most brand loyal. Marketers should focus on creating innovative new products rather than bemoan the supposed brand loyalty of an entire population.

While all those over 50 are thinking about death and dying, more of those in only one subsegment, the male Insecure, are thinking frequently of suicide. Social service agencies could plan interventions and structure programs to reach male Insecure before they carry out their plans. The factors leading to their suicides are both attitudinal and demographic.

REFERENCES

Braus, Patricia, "Mom's Monthly Mortgage Check," *American Demographics*, December 1992, pp. 48-49.

Brecht, Susan, "Selling Seniors What They Want," *Mortgage Banking*, November 1987, pp. 81-88. Source of AARP study on seniors' desire to stay in own homes.

Freedman, A. M., "The Microwave Cooks Up a New Way of Life," *Wall Street Journal*, Sept. 19, 1989, p. B1.

"Geriatric Healthcare Personal Care Products Market in the U.S.," report by Frost & Sullivan, 1989, Milford, MA.

Iida, Jeanne, "Automated Bill Payments Surge, Slashing Millions from Bank Costs," *American Banker*, May 10, 1990, pp. 1, 3.

National Center for Health Statistics, *Health: United States 1988*, 1989:74, Hyattsville, MD.

National Institute on Aging, *Special Report on Aging 1988-1989*, 1988:13, Bethesda, MD.

Peterson, Karen, "Most Elderly Don't Make Housing Plans," *USA Today*, April 5, 1990, p. D1.

"There's No Place Like Home," *Kiplinger's Personal Finance*, January 1993, p. 92. Source of studies by National Association of Realtors and National Association of Home Builders on planning to move versus actually moving.

U.S. Bureau of the Census, Current Population Reports, Series P-20, No. 456, *Geographical Mobility: March 1987 to March 1990*, U.S. Government Printing Office, Washington, D.C., 1991.

U.S. Department of Commerce, American Housing Survey, *Current Housing Reports*, December 1988, H-150-85, Washington, D.C.

Waldrop, Judith, "The Powerful Lure of Home," *American Demographics*, July 1991, p. 10. Source of Bernard Cohen's study on length of time in final area of residence.

Zelenko, Laura, "Empty Homes Get Cozy by Computer," *American Demographics*, October 1992, pp. 25-26.

TEN

POLITICS: MANY VOICES

TWO POLITICAL SCENARIOS

In an article written fifteen years ago, Betsy Gelb, a member of the marketing faculty at the University of Houston, presented two scenarios regarding demands that mature consumers would make on business. In one version, seniors, having little labor value and politically inactive, posed no problem to business. This view was predicated on the belief that seniors would not join age-specific groups.

An opposing view that Gelb outlined saw the mature population as becoming more politically aggressive for a number of reasons, including their clustering in retirement communities. In this scenario, seniors would become increasingly more militant, joining such groups as the Gray Panthers. This projection saw retirement-age persons singling out business as the focal point for their political activities.

We will show that very little of either of the scenarios that Gelb described has come to pass. Gelb's article does, however, serve as a useful framework for examining the power and politics of today's mature citizens by the 50+ segments.

In this chapter we seek to understand how politics in general, rather than any specific campaign, affects the lives of those over 50. Our results explain far more specifically and clearly the dynamics of the important mature vote during the last presidential campaign.

The gender gap that exists between all of the males and females in three of the four Self segments will be examined in this chapter. In addition, the involvement that the various segments have in political campaigns will be scrutinized, especially that of one female subsegment.

THE FINANCIAL ROOTS OF POWER

Gelb's article was written 15 years ago when about one-third of mature consumers were living in poverty. Today, the financial situation of the mature population is quite different. As outlined in Chapter 3, households headed by someone over 50 currently have a median net worth twice that of all U.S. households. Persons over 50, according to the Bureau of the Census, possess 43 percent of all spendable discretionary income.

127

Valuable workers

Because an upcoming labor shortage is predicted, the work that those over 50 can produce will become increasingly important. Our study shows that 51 percent of the over-50 population has retired at least once with no intention of returning to work. However, 57 percent of those over 50 and 11 percent of those over 65 are currently working. They have either never retired from work or have returned to work after retirement. From McDonald's to American Airlines, older workers are now on the job.

MATURE CITIZENS WIELD POLITICAL CLOUT

In terms of political impact, the influence seniors have on government spending is evident. Today one-third of the federal budget is consumed by entitlements to those over 65. Of federal social spending, 55 percent, or about $348 billion a year, goes to programs that benefit citizens over 65 who represent 12 percent of our population.

Entitlements preserved through vote

The entitlements that mature citizens have received have been preserved through both boom and bust economic cycles because seniors, unlike younger citizens, vote.

The Current Population Survey reports that in 1988 one-third of all eligible voters were not even registered. Of the remaining two-thirds, only half actually voted. Such apathy on the part of U.S. citizens overall can be contrasted with the voting records of its mature citizens, four-fifths of whom regularly vote. And voting tends to rise with age. For example, in the 1988 election, 68 percent of those between the ages of 45 and 64 voted; in contrast, only 36 percent of those 18 to 24 did so.

VOTING PATTERNS OF SELF SEGMENTS

Although seniors overall tend to vote more than do younger citizens, important differences exist among our Self segments. In our study, 82 percent of those over 50 say that they always vote in federal elections. At a rate more than would be expected, however, far more Financial Positives (90 percent) and Upbeat Enjoyers (88 percent) vote than do the Insecure (72 percent).

Voting rates differ by gender and segment

From this examination one could conclude that the wealthy Financial Positives vote more frequently and the impoverished Insecure vote least frequently. But breaking our four Self segments apart by gender shows another perspective.

In comparing males to females in each segment, 6 to 9 percent more males than females vote in three of the four segments. For example, more male Threatened Actives (86 percent) vote in every election as compared to female Threatened Actives (77 percent).

More female Financial Positives vote

The subsegment that votes at the highest rate is, however, the female Financial Positives. While 82 percent of the population over 50 says that it votes in every federal election, 95 percent of females in this segment do so. This is one example of how attitudes toward life and gender combine to affect voting patterns and political participation more than income does.

PARTY AFFILIATION BY SEGMENT

Major parties claim equal share

Which party best reflects the views of those over 50? The 50+ study shows that both Republicans and Democrats can claim the same percentage (39 percent) of identification among mature voters. Examined by segment, more Insecure (44 percent) as compared to Financial Positives (36 percent) hold the belief that the Democratic Party best represents their views. In contrast, more Financial Positives (47 percent) believe that the Republican Party best reflects their views as compared to the Insecure (33 percent) (see Figure 10–1).

Of those over 50, 10 percent overall report identifying with being independent of political parties and the same percent believes that no party reflects their views. Less than 1 percent of the mature population identifies with the Socialist, Libertarian, or other parties.

According to a survey completed by Voter Research and Surveys and reported in *The New York Times,* in the 1992 election almost equal percentages of persons 45 to 59 voted for Clinton (41 percent) than for Bush (40 percent). Perot garnered 19 percent of this age group's vote. Among those 60 and over, far more voted for Clinton (50 percent) than for Bush (38 percent). Fewer in this age group voted for Perot (12 percent) as compared to persons between 45 and 59.

Although the contrast between the Democratic-leaning Insecure and the Republican-tending Financial Positives can be dismissed as resting primarily on the immense financial differences between the two segments, breaking the segments further by gender reveals far more interesting polarities that cannot be explained away by financial resources.

MATURE GENDER GAP EXISTS

Females favor Democratic Party

Regardless of their median household income, more females in three of the study's four attitudinal segments, the Upbeat Enjoyers, Insecure, and Threatened Actives, say that the Democratic Party reflects their views (see Figure 10–2). As Cokie Roberts, the Capitol Hill correspondent for NPR and ABC, has remarked, "Older women are... the base of the Democratic Party. If a Democrat doesn't get a very strong older-woman vote, the Democrat loses." Obviously, Clinton had this vote. In the 1992 election more

Figure 10–1 Political Party Affiliation, 50+ Self Segments

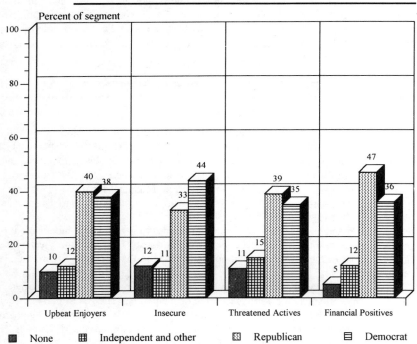

Compared to the other Self segments, more Insecure are Democrats, while more Financial Positives are Republicans. Of the four segments, more Insecure don't identify with any political party.

females 45 to 59 (43 percent) and over 60 (51 percent) supported Clinton than did males in these age groups (40 and 49 percent respectively).

Although females in the Upbeat Enjoyers, Insecure, and Threatened Active segments are solidly Democratic, they could not have been identified and grouped together solely by their demographic characteristics. For example, the median pre-tax household incomes of the females in these segments are diverse: Upbeat Enjoyers, $27,855; Insecure, under $10,000; and Threatened Actives, under $10,000. In terms of assets, the female Upbeat Enjoyers have more assets ($43,657) than do the Insecure ($17,157). Far more female Upbeat Enjoyers (34 percent) have a college degree or more as compared to the female Threatened Actives (19 percent).

One explanation for the fact that females in these three segments have bound with the Democratic Party is that, compared to the female Financial Positives, they are far less married. For example, fewer female Upbeat Enjoyers (49 percent) are married as compared to female Financial Positives (59 percent). Among the female Insecure, the very poorest segment, only 32 percent are married.

Since half of the female Upbeat Enjoyers are without a husband and possess half the assets of the Financial Positives, they may be more secure than their sisters, but still in a relatively fragile financial situation.

The larger context of their financial situation, coupled with their attitudes toward themselves and life, makes many female Upbeat Enjoyers a good fit with the Democratic Party (see Figure 10–2). Attitudinally the Upbeat Enjoyers are a very social and progressive group, believing that change is a positive thing. This segment is involved in many activities, including a high rate of participation as volunteers. It is no wonder they identify with the Democratic Party.

Figure 10–2 Political Party Affiliation, Females, 50+ Self Segments

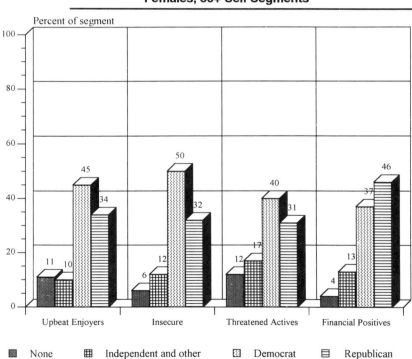

More females in three of the four Self segments are Democrats. However, more female Financial Positives identify with the Republican Party.

Financial Positives Republicans

Unlike the other three segments, the majority of female Financial Positives are Republicans, as are their male counterparts (see Figure 10–2). Admittedly, these females have an annual median pre-tax household income ($33,200) which is higher than that of the Upbeat Enjoyers ($27,855), who are predominately Democrats. But there are also differences in attitudes. Compared to the Upbeat Enjoyers, the Financial Positives see change as a far less positive force. In addition, the Financial Positives have very different attitudes toward money, investing, and retirement than do the other segments.

Males in all segments mostly Republican

Overall, males in the Self segments are more solidly Republican than their female counterparts. However, virtually equal numbers of male (33 percent) and female (32 percent) Insecure believe the Republican Party reflects their views. In addition, equal numbers of male Insecure believe the Democratic (33 percent) or Republican (33 percent) parties represent their views (see Figure 10–3).

The percentage of males in the Upbeat Enjoyer, Threatened Active, and Financial Positive segments who believe that the Republican Party reflects their views ranges from 44 to 47 percent. Although each of these segments holds vastly different attitudes toward life and aging, males in all of these segments align themselves with the Republican Party (see Figure 10–3).

Male Insecure reject political system

More males in the Insecure segment have dropped out of the political process. More of the male Insecure (22 percent), in contrast to the entire population of those over 50 (10 percent), say that no political party reflects their views (see Figure 10–3). One out of ten males in the Insecure segment say that they never vote in any federal, state, or local election as compared to one out of twenty of those over 50.

The male Insecure have the lowest annual pre-tax household income of males in any attitudinal segment ($20,793). Feeling unsuccessful and not having attained financial security, far fewer male Insecure than males in the other segments identify with our political system.

BEYOND THE VOTE

Politics doesn't draw senior volunteers

Although the majority of those over 50 vote in every election, far fewer of them take political action or communicate with their government or its representatives in other ways. For example, only 12 percent of those over 50 volunteer on political campaigns. When examined by segment, we see that more Financial Positives (15 percent) and Threatened Actives (14 percent) do so and at a rate higher than would be expected (see Figure 10–4).

**Figure 10–3 Political Party Affiliation,
Males, 50+ Self Segments**

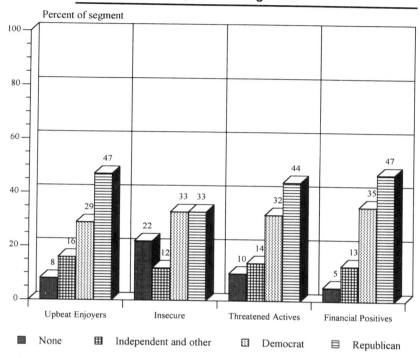

More males in all segments, except the Insecure, are Republicans. Compared with the other segments, far more male Insecure don't identify with any political party.

In addition, in every segment the female component volunteers far more than the male. For example, more female Threatened Actives volunteer frequently or occasionally (19 percent) in political campaigns than do male Threatened Actives (11 percent). Politicians interested in recruiting seniors for political campaigns would do well to concentrate their efforts on females in this segment.

Contributions differ by segment

One-quarter of the population over 50 contributes either frequently or occasionally to a political campaign. Again, when examined by gender and segment we see interesting patterns developing that could be useful to those raising funds for politicians.

It is true that both female and male Financial Positives contribute at a far higher level (33 and 31 percent respectively) than the over-50 population. However, male Upbeat Enjoyers also contribute at that level (33 percent) in contrast to female Upbeat

Enjoyers (26 percent). The number of female Threatened Actives (27 percent) who frequently or occasionally contribute to a political campaign is above that for the mature population. As we shall see below, the one potent political force among females in the four Self segments are female Threatened Actives.

Female Threatened Actives a feisty group

Asked about their support of political activities, from volunteering time to lobbying, demonstrating for senior issues to contributing financially to political campaigns, female Threatened Actives take the lead. More of them than the population over 50 of both sexes take political action. While 3 percent of the female Threatened Actives demonstrate frequently for senior issues, less than 1 percent of the over-50 population does so. Eight percent of female Threatened Actives frequently lobby for senior issues compared to 1 percent of all of those over 50.

Compared to females in segments that are better off financially, the female Threatened Actives hold their own. With a median income of under $10,000, as many female Threatened Actives (27 percent) contribute financially to political campaigns as do the far more affluent female Upbeat Enjoyers (26 percent). Whereas 19 percent of the female Threatened Actives volunteer for political campaigns, 13 percent of the female Upbeat Enjoyers do so.

By far, more of the female Threatened Actives (5 percent) are members of the Older Women's League (OWL), an advocacy group for older women, than females over 50 (1 percent).

It is not surprising that female Threatened Actives are the most militant of all the segments. An examination of their attitudes shows us that the Threatened Actives fear being controlled by government. For example, they are the only segment opposed to the retesting of older persons for driver's licenses, and their opposition is quite strong.

POLITICAL ACTIVITY AMONG MATURE VOTERS

We asked our respondents about their membership in 12 political and service organizations. Other than the American Association of Retired Persons (AARP), the remaining 11 organizations have memberships in the single digits.

Gray Panthers slight appeal

The Gray Panthers, the radical organization mentioned by Gelb, was one of the organizations for seniors in which our respondents could have claimed membership. The American Association for International Aging reported that the Gray Panthers had more than 70,000 members in 1989. Relative to the over-50 population, this organization's membership is very small. In order to reach one of their members, we would have had to triple this study's sample size.

Majority are members of AARP

The organization that claims the greatest number of persons over 50 as members is AARP. Fifty-eight percent of those over 50 say that they are active members of

Figure 10–4 Participation in Political Activities, 50+ Self Segments

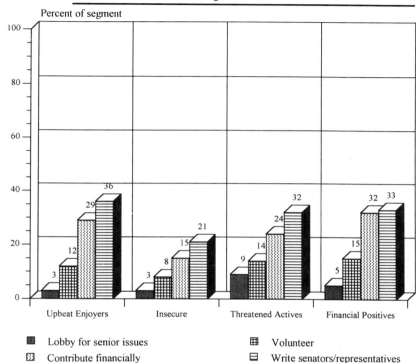

On a multiple-response question on the frequency of engaging in five political activities, more Upbeat Enjoyers "frequently" or "occasionally" write their senators or representatives. More Financial Positives contribute financially to political campaigns.

AARP. Among our Self segments, membership in this organization is concentrated in the Threatened Actives (64 percent) and Financial Positives (63 percent) segments at a rate higher than would be expected. Far fewer Insecure (51 percent) are members of AARP, although its dues are only $8 a year.

Not representing all views

Because two segments are heavily represented in AARP's membership, business-persons and social service agencies should not assume that AARP's research and reports based on its membership represent the views of all seniors. In addition, if based solely on its membership, these reports may actually present distorted views of seniors' needs simply because AARP's membership does not represent all of the 50+ segments proportionately.

Misreading its members

The debacle in 1989, when Congress repealed the AARP-backed Medicare Catastrophic Coverage Act, is one example of the fact that AARP not only does not represent the views of all seniors, it does not at times understand the motivations of its members. The Catastrophic Coverage Act was structured so that better-off taxpayers receiving Medicare would pay an income surtax to cover expanded benefits for all. A ground swell of protest rose from more affluent seniors to defeat the surtax.

AARP, unaware of the Self segments, seriously misread the interests of many of its own members and their positions. If AARP had only realized that within its membership the overly represented Financial Positives (53 percent) favored guaranteed healthcare for all citizens at a rate far below that of persons over 50 (61 percent), it may have taken a different stand.

Our 50+ study shows that more of the Insecure (69 percent) agree strongly that the United States should have guaranteed healthcare for all citizens. This support of a national healthcare program stems from the fact that three-and-a-half times as many Insecure as Financial Positives believe that they have inadequate health insurance.

Since the Financial Positives, who would have funded the program, are overrepresented and the Insecure underrepresented in AARP's membership, it is not surprising that many seniors and many of AARP's own membership fought the Medicare Catastrophic Coverage Act.

Not a militant group

Although one scenario described by Gelb suggests that seniors do not like to join groups of other older persons, AARP appears to belie that conclusion. This organization was founded in 1958. At the time Ms. Gelb's article was written in 1977, AARP was almost 20 years old and had fewer than 2 million members. At that time, 5 percent of the population over 55, then the entry age, were members of AARP. Today with 33 million members, AARP represents over half of the over-50 population.

AARP spends a great deal of its time and energy lobbying for senior issues and dealing with governmental bodies. The organization has an annual legislative affairs budget of $10 million, 18 registered lobbyists, and 125 paid political staffers. Although it is a persuasive and effective voice for the concerns and interests of seniors, AARP can hardly be viewed as militant or radical.

CONCERNS POLARIZED BY SEGMENTS

For both sexes, the four main concerns facing seniors today are decreases in the funding of Medicare, no money left in Social Security, businesses being unable to support healthcare and retirement programs, and lack of affordable housing.

For 79 percent of those over 50 in the U.S. population, a decrease in the funding of Medicare is very important. However, more of the Insecure (90 percent) hold this view in contrast to the Upbeat Enjoyers (71 percent). As household income and assets rise, fewer in each of the remaining two segments say that they rate these concerns as very important (see Figure 10–5).

Businesses being unable to fund healthcare and retirement programs is of overall concern to 72 percent of those over 50. However, concern peaks with two segments that are polar opposites in terms of income and assets: the impoverished Insecure (77 percent) and the comfortably well-off Financial Positives (75 percent) (see Figure 10–5). Because far fewer Insecure have pensions (37 percent) than do Financial Positives (64 percent), the source of their concern may relate to their own tenuous financial position rather than to the possibility of losing a pension or other benefit that they actually have.

Economic issues drive older women

Across all attitudinal segments, 5 to 30 percent more females as compared to males rate each of these governmental and social concerns as "very important." With a median pre-tax household income of $33,200, more female Financial Positives (76 percent) still rate Social Security running out of money as "very important" as compared to male Financial Positives (58 percent).

Generations in conflict

Of the eight social and governmental concerns we asked our respondents to rate, two items are in areas of potential friction between the generations. These two issues are the younger generation's dissatisfaction with supporting Social Security and family pressures caused by children having to care for their aging parents. While more of the respondents rated four other concerns as very important, the majority of those over 50 still rate the two intergenerational issues as very important.

As it becomes ever more apparent that our resources as a country will have to be parceled out more equitably or even rationed to meet the needs of all generations, we believe that these issues will become of increasing concern. At the present time, those receiving federal entitlements have not had to face reductions. If and when this occurs, we predict that intergenerational conflict will come to the forefront as an issue.

In relation to the younger generation's dissatisfaction with supporting Social Security, at the present time, 59 percent of those in the over-50 population say that this is a very important concern. We foresee that this issue will become exceedingly important in the future as a decreasing number of employees support retirees receiving Social Security.

CONCLUSION

Campaign managers can make their fund-raising and volunteer recruitment efforts more successful if they use the 50+ segments. Republicans should target over-50 males in three of the four Self segments. Females in the Financial Positive segment, who have high incomes and also belong to AARP, are good targets for Republicans.

The gender gap that exists among those over 50 is not based solely on income or assets. While females over 50 with lower incomes identify with the Democratic Party, so do many of the financially comfortable female Upbeat Enjoyers. Democrats will

Figure 10–5 Important Social and Political Issues, 50+ Self Segments

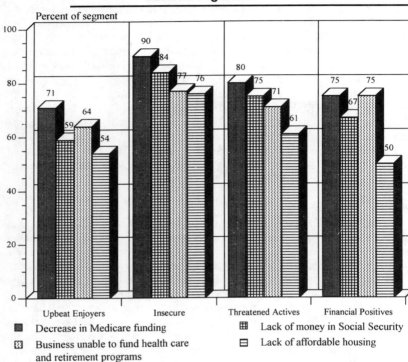

On a multiple-response question on the importance of eight issues affecting seniors, more Insecure are concerned with decreases in Medicare funding. Three-quarters of the wealthy Financial Positives are concerned about businesses being unable to fund healthcare and retirement programs.

be most successful if they understand the needs and concerns of these females, as well as those in the Insecure and Threatened Actives segments.

Marketers and politicians should not assume that because it has an immense membership base that AARP accurately reflects the needs and motivations of those over 50. Its membership is clearly skewed to two mindsets represented by the Threatened Actives and Financial Positives.

As resources become increasingly scarce, conflicts between generations should increase. The female Threatened Actives, who exhibit a militant spark, is the segment that should be watched. If their numbers grow, they may prove to be a thorn in the side of business and government.

REFERENCES

"Aging Baby Boomers: A Bigger Impact on Election Day," *Business Week*, December 16, 1991, p. 20.

Devoss, David, "28 Million Strong, AARP Is Anything but Retiring," *Star Tribune*, February 19, 1989, pp. 1E, 6E.

Gelb, Betsy, "Gray Power: Next Challenge to Business?" *Business Horizons*, April 1977, pp. 38-45.

"Money Newsline," *Money*, June 1992, p. 23.

Phil Trupp, "Capitol Hill Correspondent," *Profiles*, October 1992, p. 54. Interview with Cokie Roberts.

"Portrait of the Electorate," *The New York Times*, November 5, 1992, p. B9. Survey conducted by Voter Research and Surveys.

Smith, Lee, "What Do We Owe the Elderly?" *Fortune*, March 27, 1989, pp. 54-62.

Uebling, Mark D., "All-American Apathy," *American Demographics*, November 1991, pp. 30-35. Source of statistic from the Current Population Survey on voter apathy.

ELEVEN

WHERE AND WHAT THEY SPEND

Those who are old and poor have nothing to spend. Those who are old and wealthy won't spend. They're impossible to find, and, even if found, they aren't worth the effort. This chant is repeated over and over again by all too many retailers in reference to the mature retail customer. Their approach to this population is limited to discounts on Tuesdays and chairs installed in the ladies' restroom.

The truth about the mature consumer's shopping needs doesn't lie somewhere between or around the generalities stated above. It lies in radically new perceptions of those over 50 as groups of consumers who have diverging needs. Fresh, new strategies for pursuing the mature market will focus on attitudes, as well as behaviors and demographics.

Still good shoppers

This chapter begins with a brief consideration of the mature market's discretionary income and then details various types of retail purchases. We will see that although two segments are sufficiently affluent to spend more than the over-50 population on clothing, only one does so. The frequency of visits to various types of retail establishments is analyzed by segment.

After noting the numbers and ages of each segment's grandchildren, we outline each segment's expenditures for various types of gifts and how often they are given. Findings we would not have expected surface in our discussion of expenditures on gifts given by the Self segments.

Money to spend

According to a joint study by the Census Bureau and the Conference Board, 41 percent of those U.S. households with discretionary income are headed by someone over 50. If examined on a per capita basis, these households have more discretionary income than any other age group. In fact, households headed by someone 55 to 59 have the highest annual discretionary income: $14,584.

Mature consumers are neglected by mass merchandisers who ignore their high discretionary income. A recent study commissioned by the International Mass Retail

141

Association shows that mass merchandisers are structured to serve traditional home-makers, a group that now accounts for only 10 percent of the country's primary shoppers.

In contrast, retirees, who account for 12 percent of primary shoppers, receive little attention. This group is, in fact, the one that is growing most rapidly. Also ignored: empty nesters between 50 and 65.

RETAIL PURCHASES

Looking stylish

Concerned with looking as attractive as possible, the Financial Positives spend far more money than the over-50 population or the other Self segments on clothing. Compared to the less than $600 a year spent on clothes by those over 50, the Financial Positives estimate that they spend a median of $1,090.20. To put this number into perspective, we note that those under 50 spent an average of $594.36 per person in 1988, while the Insecure and Threatened Actives spent $452.28 and $507.72 respectively.

The Financial Positives' high clothing expenditures are, however, largely concentrated in the female subsegment. Compared to their male counterparts, who spend a median of $860.16 annually on clothing, the female Financial Positives estimate that they spend far more: $1,260. In fact, almost a quarter (22 percent) of the female Financial Positives spend $200 or more on clothing every four weeks. In comparison, only 13 percent of the population over 50 spends this much on clothing over that timespan.

Home furnishings

The Upbeat Enjoyers spend more on household furnishings each year than do the other segments. Data from our 1989 50+ study shows that the Upbeat Enjoyers estimate they spend a median of $477.01 annually on household furnishings, compared to a median expenditure of $430.78 for the over-50 population.

Upbeat Enjoyers furnish new nests

This segment's higher level of expenditures on household items can be partially explained by the fact that they are comfortable maintaining credit balances and bank loans. In addition, more Upbeat Enjoyers, as we saw in Chapter 9, move from their homes to condominiums and apartments and might buy new household furnishings at that time.

WHERE THEY SHOP

Financial Positives favor department stores

Other studies have shown that department stores appeal more strongly to older consumers than to those who are younger. Today, those over 45 account for one-third of all department store sales, and the number of retail dollars spent in department stores increases with age. For example, those 45 to 54 spend 28 percent of their retail dollars in department stores in comparison to those over 65, who spend 39 percent of their retail dollars in such stores.

Although mature consumers overall favor department stores, Financial Positives are their very best customers. In the attitudinal portion of the questionnaire, the Financial Positives agreed that they like to shop at well-established stores that they know. Our data shows that for Financial Positives, department stores fulfill this need.

More frequent visits

Those in this segment visit department stores far more frequently than do the other Self segments. According to data from our 1989 50+ study, Financial Positives visit a department store a median of four times every four weeks, or once a week. In contrast, those over 50 make a median of two visits every four weeks.

Expressed from another perspective, over half (53 percent) of the Financial Positives make five or more visits to a department store in a four-week timespan as compared to the population over 50 (32 percent). A more telling comparison is that only 36 percent of the Upbeat Enjoyers, the other affluent segment, make this number of department store visits (see Figure 11–1).

Credit card possession and usage are also indications of the Financial Positives' love affair with the department store. Of the Financial Positives, 60 percent have a department store credit card compared to 53 percent of the over-50 population.

Of all of those in the Self segments who have a department store credit card, more Financial Positives (96 percent) use their department store credit card compared to all mature consumers (92 percent). These numbers suggest that department stores do indeed fulfill the Financial Positives' need for a "well-established store."

Drug stores also a draw

More than the other Self segments, Financial Positives also make more visits to drug stores. The Financial Positives' frequent visits to drug stores may be explained by the fact that this segment spends more on personal grooming items than the others.

Of the Financial Positives, 38 percent had made over five visits to a drug store in the past four weeks. In comparison, only 30 percent of the mature population and 11 percent of the Threatened Actives had done so (see Figure 11–1).

This situation illustrates once again how averages can mislead marketers. An average fails to disclose both high- and low-frequency visitors. Target marketing becomes impossible. But distinguishing high and low usage is also insufficient for truly targeted marketing.

In terms of their attitudes, we know the Financial Positives seek value and quality. In studying their behaviors, we have seen that they are overconsumers of cosmetics and treatment products. By combining attitudes, demographics, and behaviors, we can see that the Financial Positives should be of great importance to a brand such as Cosmair's L'Oréal, which is sold in drug stores. L'Oréal delivers high-quality cosmetics and treatment products at prices far lower than those sold in department stores under Cosmair's Lancôme brand.

Financial Positives are also visiting drug stores to purchase medications. Although slightly fewer Financial Positives (23 percent) take three or more prescription drugs daily as compared to the over-50 population (24 percent), they take them for a variety of ills ranging from angina to menopausal symptoms, artery disease to high blood pressure. In addition, Financial Positives, overconsumers of vitamins, may be buying them at drug stores.

Visits to grocery store

In a study commissioned by *Supermarket Business,* persons over 50 were shown to have made about two visits to the grocery store a week during which they made a purchase. While such averages are of some use, the 50+ study shows that the number of trips to a grocery store varies among the Self segments. While 82 to 84 percent of the Upbeat Enjoyers, Insecure, and Financial Positives make five or more trips to the grocery store over a four-week period, the Threatened Actives are less frequent visitors (see Figure 11–1).

More than one out of three Threatened Actives (36 percent) makes four or fewer visits to a grocery store over four weeks. In contrast, only one out of six of the Upbeat Enjoyers, Insecure, and Financial Positives makes four or fewer visits to a grocery store over a four-week period.

Avoidance of the grocery store, for whatever reason, is concentrated in the Threatened Actives. Explanations for their infrequent visits to grocery stores—and to drug stores—could relate to the Threatened Actives' fears about unsafe neighborhoods and being crime victims, which were revealed in the attitudinal portion of the questionnaire.

The polarity that exists among the Self segments on this point—frequency of visits to grocery stores—illustrates the fact that less-than-adequate social service programs could be created if only averages and not segment-specific needs are considered.

If they consider only averages, those planning the delivery, for example, of meals or groceries to the mature population might underestimate the Threatened Actives' needs, while overestimating the needs of those over 50.

Doing it yourself

Data from the 1989 50+ study shows that 44 percent of those over 50 had made two or more visits to a hardware store over the past four weeks. But while the majority of Threatened Actives and Financial Positives (51 percent each) had made visits at this level, far fewer Upbeat Enjoyers (31 percent) had done so.

Chains of hardware stores and home-improvement centers should clearly target the Threatened Actives and Financial Positives. Because of the activities they prefer, these two segments have a need to visit hardware stores.

More Financial Positives (44 percent) garden than those over 50 (40 percent); this segment could buy its garden supplies at such stores. More Threatened Actives (31

**Figure 11–1 Visits to Drug, Department, and
Grocery Stores, 50+ Self Segments**

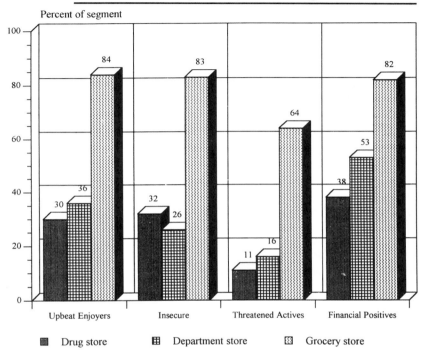

Far more Financial Positives had made five or more visits to both drug and department stores in the past four weeks. Far fewer Threatened Actives had made five or more visits to any of the three types of stores in the past four weeks.

percent) than the mature population (26 percent) select do-it-yourself projects as an activity in which they regularly participate.

GIFTS TO GRANDCHILDREN

Besides their expenditures on clothing, household furnishings, and personal grooming items, which we have discussed in this chapter and Chapter 9, the majority of those over 50 also spend money on their grandchildren. Of those in the population who are between 50 and 65, 70 percent are grandparents. The rate of being a grandparent increases to 82 percent when only those persons over 65 are considered.

To present a clearer picture of purchasing patterns, the remainder of this chapter uses only percentages based on buyers in that category. The percentages presented below, therefore, reflect only those who are category users.

Not all gift givers

First of all, not all grandparents buy gifts for their grandchildren. Of those over 50 who have grandchildren, 27 percent had spent nothing on them in the last four weeks. Those households of grandparents who do buy gifts figure that they spend a median of $650.64 annually on their grandchildren. We estimate that households with grandparents over 50 who buy gifts for their grandchildren spend $15 billion a year on those gifts.

In terms of overall gift-giving to grandchildren, the female Financial Positives give more than any subsegment. In contrast to the median of $650 spent annually by grandparents over 50 on all gifts, female Financial Positives have spent over $1,200, while male Financial Positives estimate that they spend a median of $690.72.

Clothing preferred over toys

In contrasting gifts of toys to those of clothing, within a four week period, more grandparents give clothing (73 percent) as compared to toys (65 percent). Of those who purchase toys, annual expenditures are a median of $308.28 as contrasted to a median of $567 for those grandparents over 50 who purchase clothing.

Grandparents who buy toys and clothing for their grandchildren spend almost twice as much on clothing as toys. For example, Insecure grandparents who buy such items for their grandchildren spend $246.48 on toys, but $380.16 on clothing. At the other extreme, Financial Positives who buy such items spend a median of $329.52 annually on toys, but $693.36 on clothing. The Upbeat Enjoyers who buy toys and clothing as gifts for grandchildren spend annual medians of $294.48 and $639.36 respectively. Expenditures by the Threatened Actives for such items are $334.80 and $573.24.

One indication of the weakness of using only demographics in targeting a particular market is shown by the fact that female Threatened Actives spend far more on toys for their grandchildren than any other gender-based subsegment and far more than those over 50. While the mature population spends a median of $308.28 annually on toys for grandchildren, female Threatened Actives spend $544.08. This amount is far more than that spent by the male Financial Positives ($262.20) and the female Upbeat Enjoyers ($301.08) (see Figure 11–2).

Another example occurs in examining the Self segments by gender and their clothing expenditures on grandchildren. Male Financial Positives who buy clothing for grandchildren do not spend as much as do females. Female Financial Positives spend a median of $1,071.12 annually on clothing for grandchildren as compared to males in this segment who spend $524.52, less than the national norm (see Figure 11–3).

Targeting Self segments can pay off

As we saw above, grandparents over 50 who buy in these categories spend about twice as much on clothing as on toys. These purchases are not lost on companies such as Oshkosh B'Gosh, a manufacturer of attractive, well-made clothing for infants and children. As a result of its own research, the company decided to target mothers, grandmothers, and female gift-givers over 45. Since female Financial Positives who

**Figure 11–2 Amount Spent on Toys for Grandchildren,
Males and Females, 50+ Self Segments**

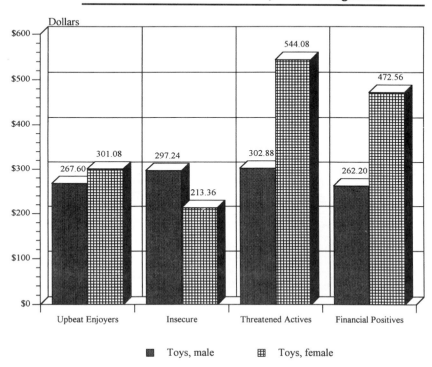

         ■ Toys, male   ⊞ Toys, female

Of those grandparents who buy toys for their grandchildren, the female Threatened Actives spent more annually than the gender-based subsegments.

buy clothing as gifts for their grandchildren spend twice as much as the national norm, Oshkosh B'Gosh would do well to target this Self subsegment.

For toy manufacturers, female Threatened Actives are clearly the subsegment to reach. Although their median incomes are low, they spend disproportionately in this category.

NUMBERS OF GRANDCHILDREN

How many grandchildren those over 50 have affects how much they spend. Because the distribution of grandchildren in the over-50 population is so polarized, it is misleading to talk about average or median numbers of grandchildren.

For example, in analyzing the numbers of grandchildren, the Insecure segment has a bimodal distribution. The word *mode* means the most frequently occurring number

Figure 11–3 Amount Spent on Clothing for Grandchildren, Males and Females, 50+ Self Segments

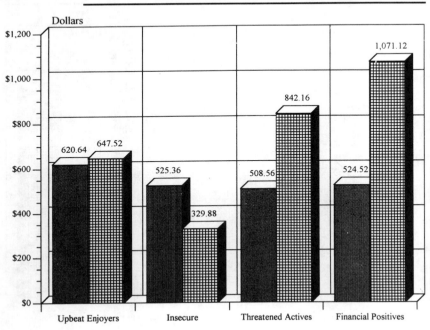

■ Clothing, male   ⊞ Clothing, female

Of those grandparents who buy clothing for their grandchildren, the female Financial Positives spent far more annually than any other gender-based subsegment. Male Upbeat Enjoyers spent more than the other male subsegments.

or percentage in a series. For the Insecure, the two modes are having no grandchildren and having four to nine of them.

Largest percentage have no grandchildren

It is important to note that the largest percentage (24 percent) of those over 50 have no grandchildren. Of the Self segments, even more Upbeat Enjoyers (27 percent) and Insecure (28 percent) have no grandchildren as compared to the national norm (see Figure 11–4).

Within each of these two segments, however, far more males have no grandchildren as contrasted with females. For example, while 19 percent of the female Upbeat Enjoyers have no grandchildren, 36 percent of the male Upbeat Enjoyers are without them. Similar percentages occur within the Insecure segment.

Two segments have more

For the population over 50, 17 percent have ten or more grandchildren. Both the Insecure and the Threatened Actives (20 percent each) have ten or more grandchildren; this is more than the over-50 population (17 percent). In the case of the Threatened Actives, far more females (28 percent) have ten or more grandchildren as compared to males (13 percent).

More Upbeat Enjoyers and Financial Positives have one to three grandchildren (32 and 31 percent respectively) (see Figure 11–4).

These specifics on the percentage of each of the Self segments that has a certain number of grandchildren give us a clearer picture than an average or median. Each segment's actual number of grandchildren is crucial in estimating expenditures on their grandchildren and in isolating and reaching those grandparents who spend the most on gifts for their grandchildren.

AGES OF GRANDCHILDREN VARY

Of those who are over 50 and who have grandchildren, most (62 percent) have grandchildren in the 4- to 12-year-old age category. However, 41 to 46 percent of the mature population also has grandchildren who are 1 to 3, 11 to 18, and over 18 years of age.

Although the median age for grandchildren has been given as 11 years of age, such a statistic is meaningless. Each Self segment tends to have more or fewer grandchildren in several age categories. Target marketing benefits from knowing these kinds of specifics, not generalities that defy application.

Examined by each of the Self segments, there is a great deal of difference in the ages of grandchildren. Although in terms of their own median age, the difference between the Upbeat Enjoyers and Insecure is only four years, there are vast differences between them in terms of the ages of their grandchildren.

Upbeat Enjoyers have younger grandchildren

At a rate higher than would have been expected, more Upbeat Enjoyers (47 percent) have grandchildren between the ages of 1 and 3. More of the Financial Positives (65 percent), who spend the most on gifts to their grandchildren, have, at a rate higher than would have been expected, grandchildren in the 4 to 12 age range (see Figure 11–5).

Insecures' grandchildren older

At the older end of the age spectrum, far more Insecure (54 percent) have grandchildren over the age of 18 as compared to the Upbeat Enjoyers (36 percent) (see Figure 11–5).

Fewer in the population over 50 (32 percent) have great grandchildren as compared to the Insecure (42 percent). Only 25 percent of the Financial Positives have great-grandchildren. More low-income Insecure, then, have not only grandchildren but great-grandchildren as well.

Figure 11–4 Total Number of Grandchildren and Great-Grandchildren, 50+ Self Segments

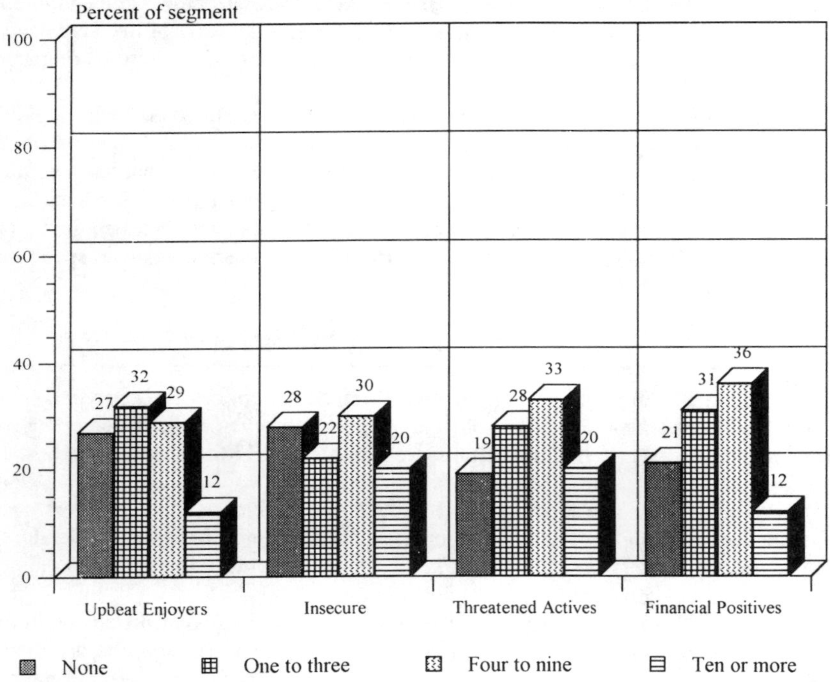

Percent of segment

| | None | One to three | Four to nine | Ten or more |

More Upbeat Enjoyers and Insecure have no grandchildren or great-grandchildren. However, more Insecure, along with the Threatened Actives, also have ten or more grandchildren or great-grandchildren.

MOST FREQUENT GIFTS

Respondents were asked to indicate how frequently they give each of 24 types of gifts to their grandchildren. Grandparents over 50 who give gifts prefer seven types of gifts. Of those gift-giving grandparents, 90 to 97 percent give greeting cards, cash, clothing, cookies and candy, meals in a restaurant, toys, and books at least once a year.

Although these seven types of gifts are the most often given, specific segments may prefer other gifts. While the affluent Financial Positives spend more on gifts for their grandchildren overall, companies should target those Self segments who prefer to give their specific products.

For example, while only 7 percent of the Upbeat Enjoyers and Financial Positives give albums, tapes or CDs as a gift five times or more per year, 18 percent of the Threatened Actives do so. In addition, while giving a grandchild movie tickets five

Figure 11–5 Age Groups of Grandchildren, 50+ Self Segments

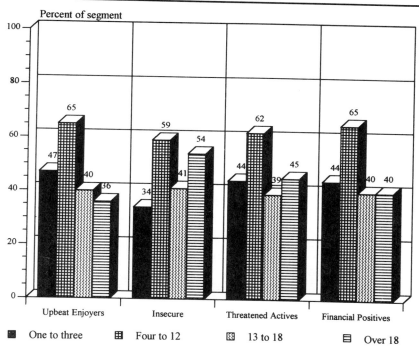

More Upbeat Enjoyers have grandchildren between the ages of 1 and 3, while more Upbeat Enjoyers and Financial Positives have grandchildren aged 4 to 12. Far more Insecure have grandchildren over 18 years of age.

times or more is done by 24 percent of both the Insecure and Financial Positives, 41 percent of the Threatened Actives give movie tickets this frequently (see Figure 11–6).

Reaching out

Although perhaps not construed as an actual present, 97 percent of those who give greeting cards to grandchildren do so once a year or more. Of the over-50 population that send greeting cards to grandchildren, 45 percent send greeting cards five times a year or more. Far more of the Upbeat Enjoyers (52 percent) as compared to any other Self segment send greeting cards this frequently to grandchildren. In contrast, 45 percent of the Financial Positives and 37 percent of the Insecure send greeting cards five times a year or more. Examined by gender, more of the female Upbeat Enjoyers

Figure 11–6 Frequency of Giving Gifts to Grandchildren, 50+ Self Segments

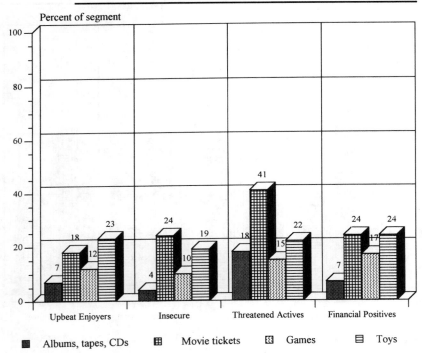

Of those grandparents who give albums, tapes, or CDs and movie tickets, more Threatened Actives give their grandchildren these items five or more times a year. More Financial Positives give games this frequently, while fewer Insecure give toys.

(58 percent) give greeting cards five times or more a year (see Figure 11–7) as compared to male Upbeat Enjoyers (43 percent).

Companies such as Hallmark and American Greetings would do well to focus on female Upbeat Enjoyers who are enthusiastic users of greeting cards. Knowing how this Self subsegment thinks about greeting cards could spawn innovative products or new ways of positioning or talking about greeting cards.

Clothing practical and popular

Of those who give clothing as a gift to their grandchildren, 93 percent give such a gift during a year's time. However, slightly more Upbeat Enjoyers and Insecure (27 percent each) give clothing as a gift to their grandchildren five times or more per year as compared to the other segments. One quarter of the Financial Positives who give gifts of clothing do so this frequently.

Figure 11–7 Frequency of Giving to Grandchildren, Females, 50+ Self Segments

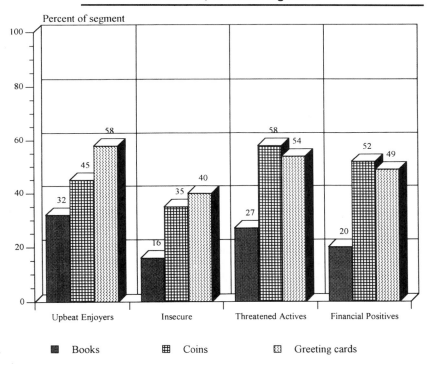

Of those grandparents who give books, greeting cards, and coins, more female Upbeat Enjoyers give their grandchildren books and greeting cards five or more times a year. More female Threatened Actives give their grandchildren coins with this frequency.

Giving a gift of clothing is especially popular among male Financial Positives, 29 percent of whom give such a gift five times or more per year. Male Threatened Actives are the least frequent givers of clothing with only 23 percent of them giving such a gift at this level of frequency (see Figure 11–8).

Examined by age, clothing as a gift declines in three of the four Self segments after 65. For example, of those Upbeat Enjoyers 65 and younger who give clothing, 33 percent do so five times a year or more as compared to 18 percent of those who are older than 65. Regardless of their age, virtually the same percentages of Insecure give clothing with this frequency.

Gifts of food

Two selections in our multiple-choice question related to gifts of food. Of those who give cookies or candy as a gift to a grandchild, 93 percent do so at least once a year or more. The Financial Positives (56 percent) are most apt to give such a gift five times a year or more.

Of those who give meals in a restaurant as a gift to a grandchild, 92 percent do so at least once a year or more. More Financial Positives and Upbeat Enjoyers (46 percent each), of those who give such a gift, do so five times a year or more. In contrast, only 36 percent of the Insecure who give meals in a restaurant do so this frequently. When examined by age, however, far more Threatened Actives over 65 (59 percent) give a meal in a restaurant as a gift five times a year or more, among those who give such a gift.

Toys popular with two segments

Although 92 percent of those who give toys as a gift to grandchildren do so once a year or more, toys are given on a more occasional basis as compared to cookies and candy, clothing, and meals in a restaurant. Almost half of those who give toys (48 percent) do so one or two times a year.

Less than a quarter (22 percent) of those who give toys as a gift do so five or more times a year. More Financial Positives (24 percent) give toys with this frequency, followed by Upbeat Enjoyers (23 percent) (see Figure 11–6). The Insecure are the least apt of all the Self segments to give a toy as a gift at this level of frequency. In terms of gender, a dramatic difference exists between male and female Upbeat Enjoyers. While 28 percent of females in this segment give a toy five times or more per year, only 18 percent of the males do so. In the Threatened Active segment, one in four females gives a toy five times or more per year in contrast to males in this segment, only one in five of whom give toys this often (see Figure 11–8).

Upbeat Enjoyers give books

While 90 percent of grandparents give a book as a gift to a grandchild at least once a year, it too is an infrequent gift. That is, 45 percent of them give a book only one or two times a year. Of the total number of grandparents who give books, 21 percent do so five times a year or more. Far more Upbeat Enjoyers (26 percent) do so as compared to Financial Positives (19 percent) and Insecure (16 percent).

Among those who give books as a gift, doing so is concentrated among female Upbeat Enjoyers. Far more of them (32 percent) do so five times a year or more (see Figure 11–7) as compared to their male counterparts (16 percent).

Fun and games

Games are given as a gift once a year or more by 84 percent of grandparents who give games at all. They are an occasional gift, however, with only 14 percent of those who give them doing so five times a year or more. More of the Financial Positives (17 percent) give games this frequently.

In three of the four Self segments, giving games as a gift declines after 65 among those who give games by approximately 5 percent. However, among the Financial Positives there is a slight increase in the giving of games by those in the older subsegment. Of those Financial Positives who give games five times or more per year,

Figure 11–8 Frequency of Giving Toys and Clothing to Grandchildren, Males and Females, 50+ Self Segments

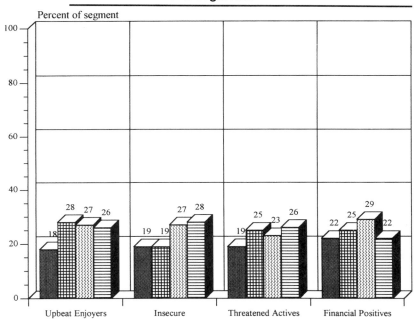

■ Toys, male   ⊞ Toys, female   ▣ Clothing, male   ⊟ Clothing, female

Of those grandparents who give toys and clothing, more male Financial Positives give their grandchildren clothing five or more times a year. More female Upbeat Enjoyers give toys this frequently.

16 percent of those 65 and younger do so as compared to 18 percent of those older than 65 (see Figure 11–9).

Money gifts vary by segment

Although they consider themselves to be savvy investors who operate with long term financial goals, the Financial Positives do not give a disproportionate amount of money-related gifts: U.S. Savings Bonds, cash, and stocks and bonds.

In terms of cash, it is given at least once a year or more by 94 percent of all grandparents who give cash. However, more of the Upbeat Enjoyers (42 percent) give cash five times or more per year as compared to the Financial Positives (35 percent). More female Upbeat Enjoyers (45 percent) than males (38 percent) who give cash as a gift do so five times a year or more.

In the case of stocks and bonds and U.S. Savings Bonds, more of the Upbeat Enjoyers, not the Financial Positives, are frequent gift givers. For example, of those who give U.S. Savings Bonds as a gift to a grandchild, more Upbeat Enjoyers (17 percent) do so five times or more per year as compared to the Financial Positives (9 percent).

Giving gifts they like themselves

Marketers should be aware of the fact that grandparents often give gifts that relate to their own interests, not necessarily those of their grandchildren. For example, in the case of coins, 82 percent of those who give them do so at least once a year or more. However, frequent givers of coins, those who give them five times a year or more, are more often Threatened Actives (45 percent) as compared to Financial Positives (34 percent). Female Threatened Actives in particular (58 percent) give coins as a gift to their grandchildren five or more times per year (see Figure 11–7). One of the Threatened Actives' favorite activities is coin collecting.

Togetherness on trips

Trips that grandparents and their grandchildren can experience together are a new travel offering from companies such as Grandtravel, located in Chevy Chase, Maryland. Our study shows that of grandparents who give vacation trips as a gift, 62 percent do so at least once a year. The two Self segments that give vacation trips as a gift three times a year or more are the Upbeat Enjoyers and Financial Positives (16 percent each), slightly more than those grandparents over 50 (14 percent) who give such a gift. Giving vacation trips five times a year or more actually increases with age.

For example, while only 3 percent of the Upbeat Enjoyers 65 and younger give grandchildren such a trip at this level of frequency, 15 percent of those over 65 do so (see Figure 11–9).

CONCLUSION

Although many of them have high discretionary incomes, some Self segments are better targets than others for specific types of products and services. Retail marketers should focus their strategies on satisfying the Self segments whose needs they can meet.

Department stores that can promise and deliver on quality and value should focus on female Financial Positives. Toy stores should try to attract female Threatened Actives. Card stores should seek their best customer: female Upbeat Enjoyers.

What the Self segments spend is related not only to their financial resources, but also to their own attitudes and needs. Although they are the wealthiest of all the Self subsegments, male Financial Positives spend no more than the national norm on their grandchildren.

In contrast, the female Threatened Actives with a far lower household income spend disproportionately on their grandchildren. While demographics are useful, they tell us only that a consumer could buy—not that he or she would buy, or why.

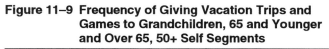

**Figure 11–9 Frequency of Giving Vacation Trips and
Games to Grandchildren, 65 and Younger
and Over 65, 50+ Self Segments**

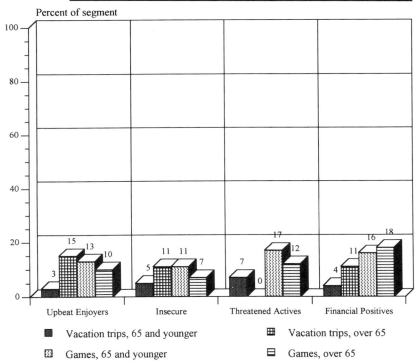

Of those grandparents who give vacation trips and games, more Upbeat Enjoyers over 65 give their grandchildren vacation trips five or more times a year. More Financial Positives over 65 give their grandchildren games this frequently.

Retailers, and the manufacturers who supply them, who are willing to establish an ongoing relationship with their customers should benefit immensely from satisfying their unmet needs. This rigorous, more demanding, approach to marketing reflects the realities of these far more competitive times.

REFERENCES

U.S. Bureau of Labor Statistics, *Consumer Expenditure Survey 1988–89*, Bulletin 2383, Washington, D.C..

"Households with Discretionary Income—Selected Income Measures: 1986," *Statistical Abstract of the United States 1991*, Table 726, p. 453.

Litwak, David, and Nancy Maline, "Competition by Class of Trade," 9th Annual Product Preference Study, *Supermarket Business,* March 1992, pp. 25-26, 35-38, 64.

"Mass Merchandisers Are Ignoring Masses of People," *Adweek,* June 1, 1992, p. 16. Source of study by International Mass Retail Association on mass merchandisers' tendency to focus on traditional homemakers.

Schlosberg, Jeremy, "Stalking the Elusive Grandparent," *American Demographics,* July 1990, pp. 33-35, 51.

Schwartz, Joe, "Will Baby Boomers Dump Department Stores?" *American Demographics,* December 1990, pp. 42-43.

Townsend, Bickley, "Fun Money," *American Demographics,* October 1989, pp. 39-41.

TWELVE

FOCUSING ON PETS

PETS BENEFICIAL AND BIG INDUSTRY

From the white toy poodle trotting happily behind an elderly woman's walker to the tortoise-shell cat purring contentedly in a little girl's lap, pets play an important role in helping us feel good. Scientific studies have shown that pets can also help us feel better. Among other things, their presence helps to lower blood pressure and reduce stress. And what is good for the general population obviously benefits those who are older.

Pet expenditures of over-50 market

But pets are not only salutary objects of our special affections, they are also big business. As a nation we spend $7 billion dollars annually on pet food and an additional $5 billion for veterinary services. If we include the cost of the pet itself, grooming, equipment, toys, clothing, and burial in a pet cemetery, expenditures on pets could easily reach $15 billion a year.

Of households over 50, 43 percent have a pet of some type. Based on our 50+ study, we estimate that these households spend $4.7 billion a year just on pet food and veterinary services. As the number of dogs continues to decrease within busy, two wage-earner families, those with money and time to care for such a demanding pet, namely those over 50, should increase in importance to manufacturers of pet foods and veterinarians.

In this chapter we will analyze what types of pets are owned by each Self segment and whether or not the ownership of specific types of pets increases or decreases by gender and age. We'll explore how pet owners rate their pets' importance to their quality of life. Next, we will take a look at how much each segment spends on its pets. Finally, we will examine where each segment buys its pet food and why it does so.

WHO OWNS A PET?

Fewer Financial Positives pet owners

Within the over-50 population, 43 percent own a pet of some type. Of the four Self segments, more Threatened Actives (46 percent) own a pet. However, even more female Threatened Actives (48 percent) than males (45 percent) do so (see Figure

159

12–1). Of the four Self segments, the segment least likely to own a pet is the Financial Positives (39 percent).

Gender affects pet ownership

Significant differences exist between two of the Self subsegments based on gender. Within the Financial Positives segment, 45 percent of the males own a pet, which is slightly above the national norm of 43 percent. In contrast, only 34 percent of the female Financial Positives own a pet. Compared to other female subsegments, fewer female Financial Positives own a pet.

The segment with the largest difference between males and females on the question of pet ownership is the Upbeat Enjoyers. While only 37 percent of the males own a pet, 50 percent of the females do (see Figure 12–1).

**Figure 12–1 Pet Ownership,
Males and Females, 50+ Self Segments**

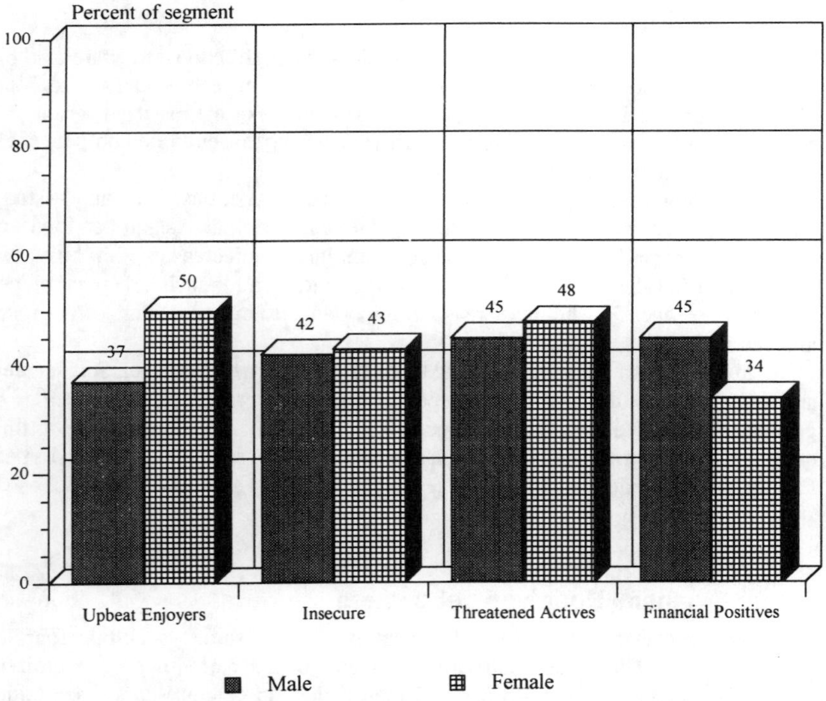

Percent of segment

Male   Female

More female Upbeat Enjoyers own pets than males or females in any other segment. Compared to the other male subsegments, more male Threatened Actives and Financial Positives own pets.

Age affects pet ownership

Age, as well as gender, impacts on the level of pet ownership. Of those between 50 and 65, 51 percent own a pet compared to 31 percent for those over 65. While three of the four Self segments are close to the national norm in terms of pet ownership after 65, far more of the older Insecure have pets (38 percent).

Interestingly, while the Threatened Actives 65 and younger have the highest level of pet ownership (59 percent), those over 65 have the lowest level of pet ownership of the four over-65 subsegments (26 percent).

TYPES OF PETS

Dogs most popular pet

People over 50 who have a pet most often cite dogs (67 percent) as their pet. Cats are owned by 48 percent of the pet owners in the over-50 population. Of those over 50 who have a pet, other types of pets are far less common: birds (7 percent), fish (6 percent), and other (4 percent).

Number of dogs owned

As we will see below, more of those in one segment or subsegment own a dog. However, no segment owns more dogs than another. When the number of dogs per 50+ household with a dog is averaged, an average of 1.3 dogs per household is the norm. This same average of 1.3 dogs per household is also found in each of the Self segments for those who own dogs.

More male Upbeat Enjoyers own dogs

While 67 percent of all pet owners over 50 own a dog, slightly more Threatened Actives (70 percent) do so. Owning a dog is highest among male Upbeat Enjoyers (76 percent) and male Threatened Actives (74 percent). In three of the four Self segments, fewer females as compared to males own a dog. In the Insecure segment, however, more females (68 percent) than males (60 percent) are dog owners (see Figure 12–2).

Female Financial Positives favor dogs

Although dogs, as a whole, are more popular with men, great differences exist within the female subsegments regarding dog ownership. For example, while half of the female Upbeat Enjoyers own a pet, fewer of them (58 percent) have dogs as compared to the other female subsegments.

In contrast, while pet ownership is low among female Financial Positives, many more of them who have a pet have a dog (70 percent) (see Figure 12–2). The female Financial Positives are highest of all the female subsegments in their level of dog ownership and exceed the national norm (67 percent).

This example illustrates the fallacy of writing marketing plans based on a generalization such as "Men prefer dogs." Overall, that is true. But for those, for example,

Figure 12–2 Dog Ownership,
Males and Females, 50+ Self Segments

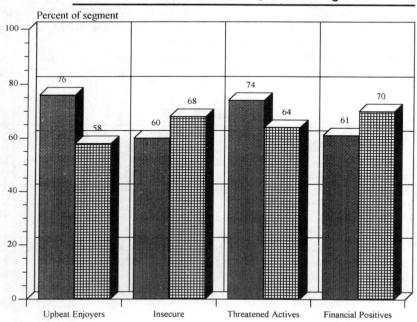

Percent of segment

	Male		Female

Of those who own pets, more male Upbeat Enjoyers own dogs than any other subsegment, male or female. Compared to the other female subsegments, more female Financial Positives are dog owners.

who are selling upscale products for dogs and need to find a specific target, female Financial Positives have to be taken into consideration.

Ownership not affected by age

In three of the four segments, dog ownership stays the same or increases with age. For example, 62 percent of the Insecure 65 and younger have a dog as compared to 71 percent of those over 65.

While dog ownership is highest among the 65 and younger Threatened Actives (74 percent), it is lowest among Threatened Actives (54 percent) over 65. Thus, the over-65 Threatened Actives have the lowest level of dog ownership of the age-based subsegments.

Cats in second place

Although cats have become more popular, those over 50, as do all U.S. households, have more dogs than cats. Unlike the average number of dogs, however, the number of cats owned by each of the Self segments differs between each segment. In the population of cat owners in households over 50, those who own cats own an average of 1.8 of them.

The average number of cats owned by Insecure and Threatened Active cat owners is higher: 1.9. Far fewer cats are owned by the Financial Positives and Upbeat Enjoyers. Cat owners in these two segments own an average of 1.5 and 1.6 cats respectively.

More Threatened Actives have cat, dog

Just as they were the segment most likely to own a dog, the Threatened Actives are also more likely to own a cat. While 48 percent of the population over 50 owns a cat, more Threatened Actives (52 percent) do so.

Sexes differ on cat ownership

When examined by gender, male Financial Positives (55 percent) are the most likely of all subsegments, male or female, to own a cat, while female Financial Positives (41 percent) are least likely of the female subsegments to do so. Cat ownership, however, falls to its lowest point among male Upbeat Enjoyers (40 percent) (see Figure 12–3).

Cat ownership drops with age

Those 50 to 65 have a higher level of cat ownership (51 percent) as compared to those over 65 (42 percent). However, this drop largely occurs in only two of the four Self segments, the Insecure (57 to 36 percent) and Financial Positives (52 to 39 percent).

Within the Upbeat Enjoyer and Threatened Actives segments, cat ownership levels are constant regardless of age.

Birds popular with Financial Positives

Bird ownership has been increasing over the past five years and there are now 13 million pet birds in the United States. While 7 percent of the population over 50 has a pet bird, they are most popular with Financial Positives (9 percent), particularly with female Financial Positives (11 percent). Their high level of bird ownership may partially explain why fewer female Financial Positives own a cat.

Fish ownership selective

A study by the American Pet Products Manufacturers Association (APPMA) found 78 million fish swimming in home aquariums. While fewer than 10 percent of all U.S. households have fish, those who have them tend to have an average of ten.

**Figure 12–3 Cat Ownership,
Males and Females, 50+ Self Segments**

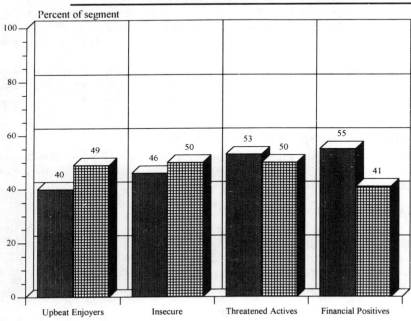

Percent of segment

☐ Male   ⊞ Female

Of those who own pets, more male Financial Positives own cats than any other subsegment, male or female. Compared to the other female subsegments, fewer female Financial Positives own cats.

Of those over 50 who are pet owners, only 6 percent own fish. The Financial Positives (7 percent) are the most likely to own fish; the Upbeat Enjoyers (4 percent) least likely. One in five fish owners over 50 has only one fish. The majority (59 percent), however, have six or more fish.

IMPORTANCE OF PETS

More pets, lower importance

While the Threatened Active segment (46 percent) has the highest level of pet ownership within the Self segments, the percentage of them (58 percent) who rate their pets as very important to their quality of life is at the same level as the national norm (59 percent).

Pets less important to Financial Positives

Far fewer of the Financial Positives (39 percent) own a pet; fewer of those who have one (51 percent) rate them as very important to their quality of life. In fact, more Financial Positives (12 percent) who have a pet as compared to the population over-50 (5 percent) report that their pets are not at all important to their quality of life.

Other two segments differ

In contrast to the Threatened Actives and Financial Positives, the majority of the Insecure (61 percent) and Upbeat Enjoyers (65 percent) report that their pet is very important to their quality of life.

While the Insecure and Upbeat Enjoyers are similar in their attitudes toward the importance of their pets, however, they are quite unalike in their demographic characteristics. The Insecure segment, for example, has the lowest median income of the four Self segments. The Upbeat Enjoyers are comfortably well-off. The Insecure are primarily widowed; the Upbeat Enjoyers are very much married.

Pets important to most females

When examining the segments by gender, females in the Upbeat Enjoyer, Insecure, and Threatened Active segments agree that their pets are very important to their quality of life at levels higher than their male counterparts. By a range of 13 to 21 percent, more females than males in these three segments rate their pets as very important. For example, 73 percent of the female Upbeat Enjoyers agree that their pet is very important to their quality of life as compared to 53 percent of their male counterparts (see Figure 12–4).

Female Financial Positives disagree

In contrast, fewer female Financial Positives (48 percent) rate their pets as very important to their quality of life compared to the other female Self segments and the over-50 population (59 percent). In addition, in the Financial Positive segment, more males (54 percent) than females (48 percent) agree that their pets are very important (see Figure 12–4).

Males downgrade importance of pets

Approximately half of the males in all four Self segments (47 to 54 percent) agree that pets are very important. These percentages are lower than the national norm (59 percent). Fewer male Threatened Actives (47 percent) rate pets as very important to their quality of life (see Figure 12–4).

Importance of pets increases with age

As many of those over 50 age, pets take on greater importance. For example, while 53 percent of the 65 and younger rate their pets as very important, 73 percent of the over 65 do so.

Figure 12–4 Importance of Pet to Quality of Life, Males and Females, 50+ Self Segments

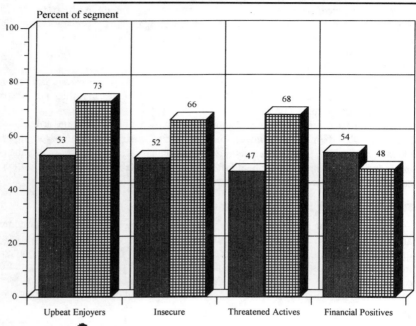

Male   Female

Of those who have pets, more female Upbeat Enjoyers rate their pets as "very important" to their quality of life than any other subsegment, male or female. Compared to the other male subsegments, fewer male Threatened Actives feel their pets are "very important" to their quality of life.

This pattern holds true for three of the four Self segments. The one exception to this pattern occurs with the Threatened Actives. Whether they are 65 and younger or over 65, almost equal numbers of them rate their pets as important (58 and 56 percent respectively).

Age variations exist between segments

Although the contribution pets make to one's quality of life rises with age for three of the four Self segments, there are wide differences between the segments on this point. On one hand, a large percentage of older Upbeat Enjoyers (88 percent) agree that their pets are very important to their quality of life. In contrast, fewer of the over-65 Financial Positives (68 percent) take this position.

SPENDING ON PETS

Upbeat Enjoyers spend more

Respondents were asked to estimate their monthly expenses for their pet or pets, including not only food but veterinary bills and toys.

The amounts that follow are all expressed as monthly median expenditures per household on a pet(s). Of all the Self segments, the Upbeat Enjoyers spend the most per household on their pets, a median of $22.94 per month compared to $19.56 by households over 50.

Although more Insecure report that their pets are important to their quality of life, they spend the lowest amount on their household's pets, a median of $16.31 per month. One explanation for this is that the Insecure are the poorest among the Self segments and can't afford to spend more on their pets—even if they want to. In contrast, the Financial Positives, who give the lowest rating for their pets' contribution to their quality of life, spend the second highest amount per household on their pets: $20.47.

Expenditures differ by gender

When examining the segments by gender, we see that, with the exception of the female Financial Positives, all the male subsegments spend more than their female counterparts. Households with female Financial Positives spend a median of $22.80 per month on pets, more than is spent by male Financial Positives ($21.50).

The female Financial Positives also spend more than the other female subsegments. At a median expenditure of $15.55 per month, households with female Threatened Actives spend the least amount on pets of the gender-based subsegments.

Households with male Upbeat Enjoyers spend a median of $24.72 per month, the most of any gender-based subsegment. Their expenditures contrast to those of the male Insecure ($20.56 per month), who spend the least of the male subsegments on their pets (see Figure 12–5).

Spending on pets decreases with age

Those 65 and younger in all of the Self segments spend more on their pets than do the over-65 subsegments. Of those 65 and younger, the Upbeat Enjoyers spend the most ($24.79 per month) and the Threatened Actives spend the least per month (a median of $17.69) on pets.

Of those over 65, the Upbeat Enjoyer segment also spends the most. However, the amount they spend at this age drops considerably to a median of $20.62. The over-65 Insecure ($14.50 per month) spend the least.

WHERE THEY BUY PET FOOD

Supermarket primary source

Respondents were given a question listing six sources of pet food. They were asked to select one of them as the place where they usually purchase food for their pet(s).

**Figure 12–5 Median Monthly Expenditures on Pets,
Males and Females, 50+ Self Segments**

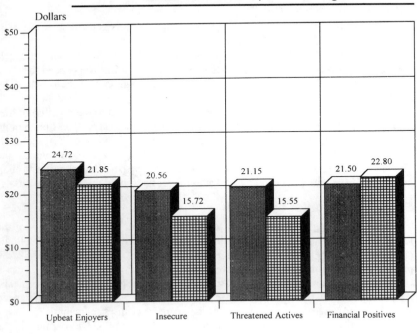

☐ Male   ⊞ Female

Of all the subsegments, male Upbeat Enjoyers spend the most on their pets each month, while female Insecure and Threatened Actives spend the least. Only in the Financial Positives segment do females spend more on their pets than males.

The population over 50 overwhelmingly buys pet food at the supermarket (78 percent).

These percentages reflect the findings of a study conducted in 1990 for the APPMA, which showed that 75 percent of all dog owners and 80 percent of cat owners bought their pets' food at a supermarket. Of the Self segments, however, the Financial Positives (73 percent) are the least apt to buy their pet food at a supermarket.

Other sources of supply

Considering that the vast majority of those over 50 buy pet food at a supermarket, other alternative sources are used far less frequently. These range from a veterinarian, where pet owners can buy a brand such as Hills, to mail order, a type of distribution used by Carnation's Perform brand.

Pet store alternative

Although only 12 percent of the over-50 population select a pet store as their primary source of supply for pet food, 17 percent of the Financial Positives do so, a larger percentage than the other three segments. However, one in four male Financial Positives select a pet store as their source of supply.

Other subsegments who favor a pet store as a source of pet food are the female Insecure (14 percent) and the male Upbeat Enjoyers (15 percent).

Veterinarian selected by some

Overall, only 7 percent of those over 50 list the veterinarian as their primary source of supply for pet food. Female Upbeat Enjoyers (14 percent) and male Insecure (13 percent) are more likely than their counterparts to buy pet food from the veterinarian.

A missed opportunity

Although buying pet food through direct mail would seem to be a convenience, particularly for those who are sick or disabled, no pet owner in the 50+ study reported buying pet food this way.

WHY THEY BUY

Convenience most important

Given a choice of eight alternatives, respondents were asked to make one selection as to why they buy pet food from their particular source. More of the over-50 population (48 percent) select convenience as the reason for doing so. Since three-quarters of pet owners over 50 buy their pet food at a supermarket, they must perceive it as sufficiently convenient.

Price also consideration

For another 17 percent of pet owners over 50, price is the most important reason for purchasing pet food from a particular source. Price is especially important to the Threatened Actives (22 percent) (see Figure 12–6). Their price-consciousness may explain why the Threatened Actives are the least likely of the Self segments to buy pet food from a veterinarian or pet store, two more expensive sources.

Other reasons noted

A pet food's higher quality or a veterinarian's recommendation are two additional reasons why those over 50 buy pet food where they do. These two reasons were selected by 11 and 7 percent respectively of the mature population. More Financial Positives (15 percent) selected higher quality (see Figure 12–6) and recommended by veterinarian (10 percent) as compared to those over 50.

Buying pet food specific for a health condition (6 percent), a breed (5 percent), a life stage (4 percent), or one with more vitamins and minerals (3 percent) were reasons

**Figure 12–6 Top Three Reasons for Buying Pet Food
from Primary Source, 50+ Self Segments**

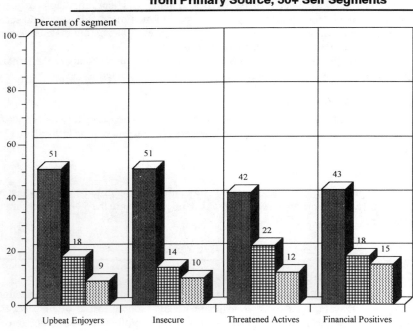

While all segments report convenience as their top reason for buying pet food from their primary source, more Upbeat Enjoyers and Insecure do. More Threatened Actives buy food from their primary source due to price, while more Financial Positives do so because of quality.

selected by small percentages of those over 50 to explain why they purchase pet food where they do.

WHAT THEY FEED

Majority feed dry food

In a multiple-choice question offering 10 alternatives, 88 percent of pet owners over 50 said that they feed dry food. More of the Threatened Actives (92 percent) feed their pets dry food, the highest of the four Self segments.

Wet food popular option

While wet food is fed to pets by 56 percent of pet owners over 50, more Upbeat Enjoyers (61 percent) do so. The other three segments are close to the national norm in terms of how many of them feed wet food.

Perhaps more Upbeat Enjoyers buy the expensive wet food than the other segments not only because they have the second highest incomes, but also because they are second in reporting that their pets are important to their quality of life.

Homemade food a choice for some

Although 17 percent of those over 50 feed their pets homemade, fresh foods, more of the Threatened Actives (25 percent) do so. This segment, which has the second lowest median income, may serve these foods because they are less expensive.

The semimoist alternative

More Upbeat Enjoyers (15 percent) and Financial Positives (14 percent) buy semimoist pet food as compared to those pet owners over 50 (11 percent). Convenience may motivate these two segments, which spend the most on their pets, to purchase this more costly pet food option.

Poor segments buy more superpremium

The Insecure (12 percent) and Threatened Actives (11 percent) are the two segments most likely to buy superpremium pet food as compared to those over 50 (8 percent). Although these two segments report both the lowest incomes and the lowest spending on their pets, more of them buy the best quality pet food. At least for the Insecure, their motivation for doing so may lie in the fact that more of them feel that their pets are very important to their quality of life.

Upbeat Enjoyers may have older pets

More than the over-50 population (5 percent), the Upbeat Enjoyers (8 percent) are more likely to buy pet food for a specific health condition. In addition, greater numbers of Upbeat Enjoyers (12 percent) buy a "light" brand of pet food as compared to pet owners over 50 (5 percent).

Targeting pet owners by segment

While the affluent Financial Positives spend the second highest amount on their pets, they have fewer of them. Other Self segments may prove to be better markets for pet-related products and services.

Although they do not have the greatest number of pets, the Upbeat Enjoyers, even as they age, continue to spend the most on their pets of all the Self segments. More Upbeat Enjoyers buy their pet food at a supermarket, but pet stores and veterinarians are also favored by male or female Upbeat Enjoyers. Both of these sources of supply could consider marketing directly to the Upbeat Enjoyers.

Information, activities resource

In attempting to reach the segment that is committed to exercise, a pet store could offer brochures or seminars on how pet owners can exercise themselves along with their pets. Because Upbeat Enjoyers have a high rate of volunteerism, a pet store could serve as a conduit for information on programs that take pets on visits to hospitals and nursing homes. These types of promotions would appeal to the Upbeat Enjoyers.

New packaging, new products

More than the other segments, the Upbeat Enjoyers prefer wet pet food and "light" foods. Where such preferences exist, manufacturers of pet foods and dog biscuits could explore the possibility of new products, packaging, or portions that appeal to one or more of the Self segments.

While the Insecure feel that their pets contribute significantly to their quality of life, their median household expenditures on their pets are the second lowest. However, a fair number of Insecure are spending beyond what their median expenditures suggest and doing so at pet stores and with veterinarians. What services and information can this segment use?

CONCLUSION

Given the ferocious level of competition that exists in a slow-growth industry, innovative marketers at companies that manufacture pet food should view those over 50 as a worthwhile target. Those who sell, groom, and care for pets should more closely examine how they can fulfill the needs of mature pet owners.

Because over-50 pet owners buy a significant portion of pet food, supplies, and services, marketers who learn what each Self segment wants and fulfill these needs will come out ahead.

REFERENCES

Crispell, Diane, "Pet Sounds," *American Demographics,* May 1991, pp. 40-44, 53. Source of study by the American Pet Products Manufacturers Association (APPMA).

Donahue, Michael, "Ownership of Birds as Pets Soars," *Star Tribune,* October 7, 1989, p. 3E.

THIRTEEN

REACHING THE SELF SEGMENTS

DEMYSTIFYING BRAND LOYALTY

The common stereotype is that mature buyers, having just gargled with Listerine, will go to their graves driving an Oldsmobile and clutching a box of Kellogg's Corn Flakes. Forget about switching them to General Mills' MultiGrain Cheerios or Toyotas or Plax. Promotional dollars are, therefore, showered on those 18 to 35, youngsters whose brand loyalties are malleable enough to be shaped.

Whether or not marketers spend advertising dollars on the over-50 population hinges on accepting their supposed unswerving loyalty to certain brands. Is it worth advertising to the mature customer if he or she is unwilling to switch? Will seniors change brands under any circumstances? If they will, what can be done and said to accomplish this end?

To answer these questions, we begin this chapter on reaching the Self segments with an examination of the mature market brand loyalty myth. We continue on with a detailed look at the most appropriate media to use in reaching each of the Self segments. This chapter contains an analysis of the Self segments' direct marketing purchases, including frequency and amount spent. The chapter concludes with suggestions on selecting direct marketing lists based on correlations with each segment's attitudes, demographics, and behaviors.

Older versus younger consumers

In discerning brand loyalty between younger and older consumers, Mark D. Uncles and Andrew S.C. Enrenberg studied a year's worth of mid-1980s purchasing records from the Market Research Corporation of America's (MRCA) national consumer panel. Reviewing sample sizes of approximately 6,000 in each of seven product categories, the authors found that the "somewhat smaller number of brands bought by older households is due in part to them buying less often . . . compared with . . . younger households." Over a longer time period, "older households would buy as often . . . [and] then have as wide a repertoire of brands as do younger ones."

The authors conclude that decreases in consumption of a product, such as salad dressing, indicate not an "inflexibility of brand choice behavior," but, rather, the

173

reduced needs of an empty nest. If consumption and brand loyalty are measured not by household, but rather by person, those over 50 are no more brand loyal than are younger consumers. This conclusion underscores the fact that it is, indeed, of value to advertise to the mature market.

No average level of brand loyalty

But beyond this fundamental conclusion, the question of brand loyalty, whether in reference to the mature market or to younger consumers, is a complex one that cannot be dismissed by simple generalizations. Our 50+ study shows that variations in brand loyalty exist both across attitudinal segments and in reference to specific products. We defined *brand loyalty* as the purchase of only one or two brands in a specific category.

Threatened Actives most brand loyal

As we will see in Chapters 17 and 22 on promotions for reaching the Health and Food segments, each attitudinal segment's brand loyalty varies according to the product itself. These segments are not equally loyal to all categories of products or to specific products within these categories.

While more of the Threatened Actives show themselves to be more consistently brand loyal than the other Self segments, their level of loyalty rises and falls depending on the product. While this segment is, for example, the most brand loyal to gasoline, hair dye, and cake mix from a box, it is only average in its loyalty to cereal and frozen dinners.

In contrast, even when Financial Positives are overconsumers in a particular product category, they reveal themselves to be the least brand loyal of all the Self segments.

Do brands deliver value?

The question of brand loyalty among the mature population doesn't rest on demographic characteristics, but on attitudes toward the values and benefits that a brand represents. Each of our segments values brands to a greater or lesser degree, and there are additional variations in loyalty to specific products.

The complexity of the situation is illustrated by the brand loyalty of category users of gasoline among the Self segments. Almost half (48 percent) of the Threatened Actives buy only one brand of gasoline as compared to the Financial Positives (36 percent), although both segments have above average levels of consumption. In fact, the Financial Positives have the lowest level of brand loyalty to gasoline of all the Self segments (see Figure 13–1).

In another product area, hair dye, more of the Insecure are category users (34 percent); however, their loyalty to one brand is slightly less than average (77 percent). Although far fewer Threatened Actives (28 percent) use hair dye, more of them (83 percent) buy only one brand (see Figure 13–1).

The high usage of hair dye among the Insecure isn't surprising. In the attitudinal portion of the study, the Insecure show themselves committed to dyeing their hair to cover gray. While they may have been dyeing their hair for twenty or thirty years, they may very well not have been using the same brand.

Among category users of cereal over 50, one in five buys only one brand. While more Financial Positives (97 percent) are category users, however, they have the lowest level of loyalty (15 percent), however, to one brand. In contrast, slightly fewer Insecure are category users (95 percent), but more of them buy only one brand (23 percent) (see Figure 13–1).

Loyalty depends on product

As the above examples show, the extent of brand loyalty varies by segment and by product and is driven by the expectations that each segment has of that product. For example, more Financial Positives (60 percent) use face cream for dry skin; however, fewer of them are loyal to one brand (63 percent). In contrast, fewer Threatened Actives (51 percent) use such creams, but more are loyal to one brand (66 percent) (see Figure 13–1).

That more Financial Positives use such creams parallels a finding from the attitudinal portion of the questionnaire. There the Financial Positives revealed themselves to be far more interested than the other Self segments in creams that would make their skin look younger. The Financial Positives' commitment to such creams may very well drive them to continually search for an ever-better product. This quest could open up opportunities for cosmetics firms within this affluent, high-use, but low-loyalty, segment.

Creating new loyalties

Beyond existing brand loyalties, however, the larger question is whether marketers of bathtubs and cake mixes, mutual funds and aerobic classes will reformat existing products and services so that large numbers of those in the Self segments will try them—and return again. New products that are distinctly different have the opportunity to create entirely new loyalties.

One innovator in the financial services industry is Charles Schwab, the discount brokerage house. Rather than bemoan the fact that many of those over 50 are buying no-load mutual funds and bypassing brokers, this firm developed two new services. One is a no-fee IRA, the other is the ability to offer scores of no-load mutual funds and attract mature investors.

A very old product, such as Crisco, might get mature consumers to switch back through entirely new packaging. Because most mature consumers live in small households, individually wrapped Crisco Sticks are more convenient than a five-pound can. A truly innovative product, Stat-One Hydrogen Peroxide Gel, could replace liquid hydrogen peroxide in the medicine cabinets of mature buyers. It is easier to apply in just the right spot.

In the highly competitive lodging business, Ramada's new Best Years Program, which offers mature travelers a 25 percent discount off a hotel stay, is certain to garner new loyalties and return visits. Those who are over 60, or are members of the American Association of Retired People (AARP), are eligible for the program.

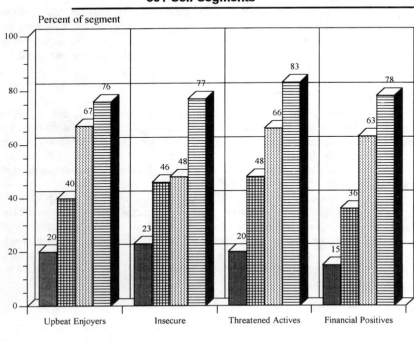Chapter Thirteen

**Figure 13–1 Brand Loyalty,
50+ Self Segments**

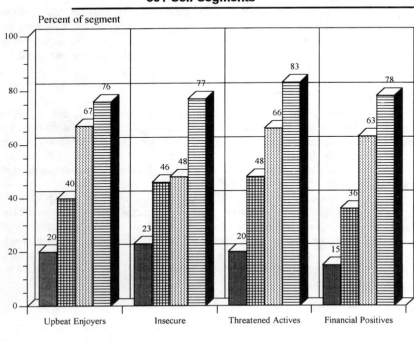

Percent of segment

Legend: ▨ Cereal   ⊞ Gasoline   ⊠ Face cream   ⊟ Hair dye

On a multiple-response question on the number of brands bought in eight product categories, more Threatened Actives who are category users buy only one brand of gasoline and hair dye. More category users among the Insecure buy only one brand of cereal.

It's evident that some companies and their marketers are developing products and services designed specifically for the mature consumer, or appropriate for over-50 consumers and others as well. Marketers who accept the fact that certain attitudinal segments within the over-50 market will try new brands should advertise to them. Selecting the promotional tools that best reach the target segment is next.

BUYING MEDIA USING ATTITUDINAL SEGMENTS

In the past, buying media by attitudinal segments or structuring promotional campaigns around them has been dismissed as a pipe dream. Attitudes were measured and segments then created based on them, but researchers didn't go on to link these attitudinal segments to list purchases, promotions, public relations or media buys. This chapter shows that all promotions can be integrated using attitudinally based segments, specifically the 50+ Self segments.

While basing promotional activities solely on demographics may be convenient, we suggest that it is also potentially wasteful. In buying media in the conventional fashion, thousands, if not millions, of people are reached who have no interest in your product.

In our studies we continually see statistically significant linkages between attitudinal segments that prefer both a specific product or brand and a certain medium or type of promotion. Buying media and creating promotions based on these relationships offer the greatest efficiencies. In addition, the images used in the advertising should reflect a segment's activities, concerns, and needs.

Selecting favored medium

Our 50+ study shows that the Upbeat Enjoyers, compared to the population over 50, are average consumers or underconsumers of every type of media. In contrast, the Insecure strongly favor network and cable television. The Financial Positives' preferred medium is newspapers. The Threatened Actives exhibit an above-average interest in radio.

TELEVISION VIEWING

Insecure prefer television

Of all the Self segments, the Insecure watch the most hours of television per week. More of this segment (58 percent) watches 11 or more hours of network television per week as compared to those over 50 (52 percent). The Insecure are also heavy consumers of cable television. More of them watch cable 11 or more hours per week (40 percent) as compared to the population over 50 (39 percent). Far fewer Upbeat Enjoyers consume 11 or more hours per week of both cable and network television (32 and 46 percent respectively) (see Figure 13-2).

What segments watch

Of the 13 programming options presented in the 50+ questionnaire, the three types of television shows most watched by those over 50 either daily or several times a week are news and current affairs (86 percent), game shows (47 percent), and talk shows (38 percent). But marketers who wish to reach a specific segment will select programming that reflects that segment's interests.

The Insecure are clearly big fans of game shows. More Insecure watch such programs (54 percent) as compared to the population over 50 (47 percent). In addition, far more Insecure (38 percent) regularly watch soap operas compared to the mature population (26 percent).

Although network television is not a preferred medium for them, more Financial Positives watch sports programs (42 percent) as compared to the mature population (36 percent) (see Figure 13-3). For almost all types of television programming, fewer Upbeat Enjoyers are regular viewers.

Figure 13–2 Media Usage,
50+ Self Segments

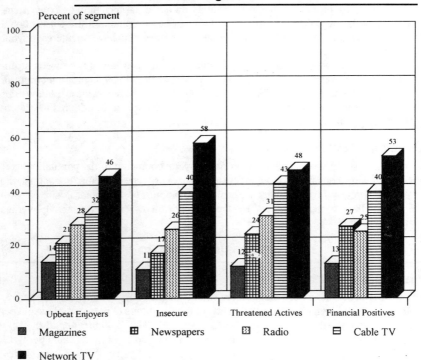

On a multiple-response question on the frequency of use of six types of media, more Insecure report spending 11 or more hours a week watching network television. More Threatened Actives spend that amount of time per week watching cable television and listening to the radio.

NEWSPAPER READERSHIP

Financial Positives favor newspapers

Newspapers are the preferred medium of the Financial Positives who spend more time each week reading newspapers than do the other segments. Compared to those over 50 (22 percent), more of the Financial Positives (27 percent) spend 11 hours or more a week reading newspapers. In contrast, fewer Insecure (17 percent) and Upbeat Enjoyers (21 percent) spend that much time each week reading newspapers (see Figure 13–2).

Segments attracted to different sections

Specific sections of a newspaper attract certain segments more than others. An automobile manufacturer that places an advertisement in the car or motoring pages of a newspaper would like knowing that more of the Financial Positives (19 percent) will be reached as compared to those over 50 (15 percent) (see Figure 13–4). As we mentioned in Chapter 6 on cars, more Financial Positives intend to buy a new car within the next two years than the over-50 population.

Besides the food, travel, and business sections, more Financial Positives than the other three Self segments are also reading the home section and personal advice columns. More male Financial Positives (68 percent) are reading the sports pages, as compared to the over-50 population (41 percent).

Reading coupon and advertising sections

More Threatened Actives (36 percent) and Financial Positives (35 percent) are reading advertising as compared to the over-50 population (32 percent). Fewer Upbeat Enjoyers and Insecure (32 percent each) read these sections.

Within the gender-based subsegments, more female Financial Positives (70 percent) and female Threatened Actives (72 percent) are reading the coupon sections of a newspaper at a rate equal to or slightly higher than the over-50 population (58 percent).

Although, as we have seen, the Financial Positives and Threatened Actives are very different in their levels of brand loyalty, they may be reading advertisement and coupon sections in order to find good values.

In the attitudinal portion of the questionnaire, which we described in Chapter 1, the well-off Financial Positives had the highest level of agreement with the statement that they look for "good values when they shop."

With the second-lowest household income of the four Self segments, the Threatened Actives may be reading advertisement and coupon sections to find the lowest price and highest value. In the attitudinal portion of the questionnaire, the Threatened Actives were the only segment that wanted to get discounts because of its age. In addition, the Threatened Actives also seek out long-lasting products.

SELECTING MAGAZINES BY SEGMENT

Although many magazines offer very similar demographics, our study shows that some magazines are better than others in reaching specific 50+ segments. A manufacturer of exercise machines, such as NordicTrack, should target the Upbeat Enjoyers, a segment committed to exercising and staying in shape, in the magazines they prefer.

This approach is more efficient than advertising in scores of publications and using trial-and-error to select a list of media that work. In the throw-it-against-the-wall-and-see-if-it-sticks approach, thousands, if not millions, of dollars are wasted.

Measuring magazine readership

Unlike other measures of readership, our 50+ study defined readership more narrowly. The term *reader,* as we have used it here, refers to either the purchaser or subscriber of a magazine, or a respondent who lives in a household where the magazine is regularly available through subscription or purchase.

Figure 13–3 Television Programming Watched, 50+ Self Segments

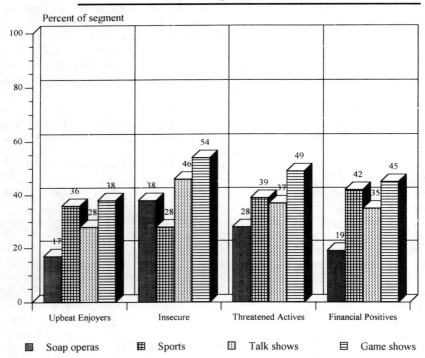

On a multiple-response question on the frequency of watching 13 types of television programs, more Insecure watch soap operas, talk shows, and game shows several times a week or more. More Financial Positives view sports several times a week or more.

Upbeat Enjoyers heavy readers

Marginal television viewers, the Upbeat Enjoyers are slightly above average in the number of hours they spend reading magazines. For example, 14 percent of the Upbeat Enjoyers report reading magazines from 11 hours or more a week. In comparison, those over 50 and the Financial Positives (13 percent each) spend this amount of time per week reading magazines (see Figure 13–2).

Multiple magazine readers

The Magazine Publishers of America (MPA) defines a magazine reader as one who regularly reads five magazines. Five publications are most popular among the persons in the Self segments who fit the MPA's definition of a magazine reader: *Reader's*

Figure 13–4 Newspaper Sections Read, 50+ Self Segments

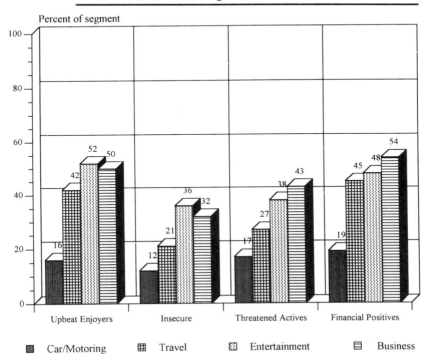

Percent of segment

Upbeat Enjoyers   Insecure   Threatened Actives   Financial Positives

▓ Car/Motoring   ⊞ Travel   ▨ Entertainment   ⊟ Business

On a multiple-response question listing 20 sections of the newspaper, more Financial Positives than the other segments regularly read the car/motoring, travel, and business sections. More Upbeat Enjoyers regularly read the entertainment section.

Digest (68 percent), *Better Homes & Gardens* (54 percent), *Good Housekeeping* (47 percent), *Family Circle* (46 percent), and *Ladies' Home Journal* (36 percent).

More of the Financial Positives (33 percent) and Upbeat Enjoyers (31 percent) can be classified into the MPA's definition. As we have seen, however, a higher percentage of Upbeat Enjoyers spend more time reading magazines than do the Financial Positives. Examples given below illustrate that even with these readers of multiple magazines, specific publications appeal to each segment.

Reaching the Upbeat Enjoyers

Family Circle is a good bet in planning media campaigns to reach more of the female Upbeat Enjoyers (32 percent) than the over-50 population (22 percent). Among multiple magazine readers, even more Upbeat Enjoyers (53 percent) regularly read *Family Circle* as compared to those over 50 (46 percent).

More male Upbeat Enjoyers (29 percent) can be targeted through *National Geographic* than the population over 50 (19 percent). Another option is *Smithsonian,* which more male Upbeat Enjoyers (14 percent) read than the mature population (8 percent) (see Figure 13–5). Among multiple magazine readers, *Smithsonian* is read by more Upbeat Enjoyers (23 percent) than the mature population (19 percent).

At a rate higher than would be expected, more Upbeat Enjoyers also read *Midwest Living, Business Week,* and the *New York Times Magazine.*

Financial Positives prefer *Reader's Digest*

Reader's Digest enjoys a higher level of readership among the Financial Positives (50 percent) than among the mature population (46 percent). Among multiple magazine readers, *Southern Living* attracts more Financial Positives (22 percent) than persons over 50 (17 percent).

Money is read by more Financial Positives (10 percent) than the over-50 population (6 percent). Certainly sellers of financial products should know that an even greater percentage of female Financial Positives who are multiple magazine readers regularly read *Money* magazine (17 percent). These females have assets, excluding their homes, of $79,585 compared to $43,743 for the population over 50.

At a rate higher than would be expected by chance, more Financial Positives also read *Lear's, Sunset,* and *Better Homes & Gardens.*

SENIOR OR MAINSTREAM PUBLICATIONS?

A question facing those companies that want to advertise to the mature market is whether to approach it in general, mainstream publications, such as *Reader's Digest,* or in magazines such as *Modern Maturity* and *New Choices for Retirement Living,* which target the mature market specifically.

The case for *Modern Maturity*

Of those over 50, 58 percent are members of the American Association of Retired Persons (AARP) and receive its publication, *Modern Maturity.* An impressive 52 percent of our sample reports reading *Modern Maturity* regularly. The circulation of *Modern Maturity* is so immense it dwarfs that of other senior publications.

From our study, however, we can show that some Self segments believe *Modern Maturity* is doing a better job than others. To begin with, far more of the Financial Positives (58 percent) read the publication regularly as compared to the Insecure (48 percent) and the over-50 population (52 percent).

Two-thirds of its readership believe the publication delivers useful health information. However, 71 percent of the Financial Positives share this view. On two other measures, more Financial Positives and Upbeat Enjoyers agree that *Modern Maturity* delivers useful financial and lifestyle information. On every measure, the Insecure and the Threatened Actives are the Self segments least satisfied with *Modern Maturity* (see Figure 13–6).

Figure 13–5 Magazines Read,
Males, 50+ Self Segments

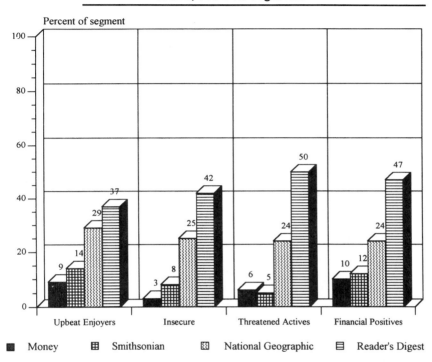

On a multiple-response question listing 39 magazines, more male Upbeat Enjoyers report reading *Smithsonian* and *National Geographic*. More male Financial Positives read *Money*, while more male Threatened Actives read *Reader's Digest*.

Other options reach seniors

There is no simple answer as to where to advertise to the mature market. While it is true that *Reader's Digest* is read by 50 percent of the Financial Positives, 58 percent of them read *Modern Maturity*. However, advertising in *Reader's Digest* reaches Americans under 50 as well.

In advertising to the mature market, another option is to select a publication formed around a particular product or service, for example, home, financial, or travel, which has a base of older subscribers. Some publications in this area are *Kiplinger's Personal Finance Magazine* and *Smithsonian*. The median age of subscribers to *Smithsonian* is 49.6. Its subscribers have a median household income of $53,500. Subscribers to *Kiplinger's Personal Finance Magazine* have a median age of 58 and a median household income of $53,700.

Figure 13–6 Satisfaction with *Modern Maturity*, 50+ Self Segments

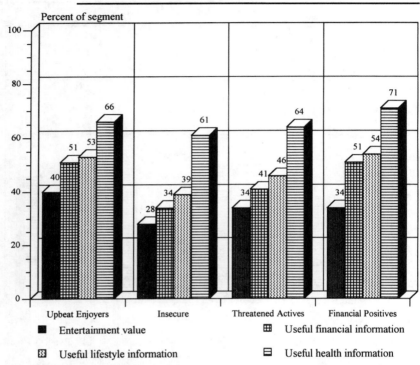

On a multiple-response question on the usefulness of *Modern Maturity* magazine, more Financial Positives who are readers report that it provides useful lifestyle and health information. More Upbeat Enjoyers believe it has entertainment value.

TUNING IN TO RADIO

Threatened Actives listen most

More Threatened Actives (31 percent) listen to radio 11 hours or more per week than the national 50+ population (27 percent). Fewer Insecure and Financial Positives (26 and 25 percent respectively) listen to radio at this level. Slightly more Upbeat Enjoyers (28 percent) invest this much time listening to radio each week (see Figure 13–2).

Segments have favorites

At a significant level the Threatened Actives and Insecure (41 and 40 percent respectively) listen to country music on the radio far more than do the Upbeat Enjoyers (30 percent) or the population over 50 (36 percent).

Although not overconsumers of radio, the Upbeat Enjoyers use it as a musical resource, with the exception of country music. This segment (56 percent) listens to easy listening more than the over-50 population (50 percent). In addition, more of them (34 percent) listen to classical music than does the mature population (21 percent) (see Figure 13–7). More than the other segments, the Upbeat Enjoyers also listen to jazz and rock on the radio.

IMAGES FOCUS ON ACTIVITIES

Advertising targeted at a specific 50+ Self segment should show them engaged in some of their favorite activities. For the Upbeat Enjoyers some of the activities in which they participate regularly at rates higher than those in the over-50 population include book reading (47 percent), children (41 percent), cultural and art events (25 percent), and photography (16 percent).

More Financial Positives than would be expected list watching sports on television (52 percent), gardening (44 percent), stocks and bonds (22 percent), and golf (17 percent) as some of their top activities.

As compared to the over-50 population, more of the Threatened Actives regularly engage in do-it-yourself projects and home-workshop activities (31 percent), coin and stamp collecting (9 percent), and hunting and shooting (12 percent). Only two activities, housework (50 percent) and sewing (26 percent), occur within the Insecure segment at rates higher than we would have expected.

Tying activities into ads and promos

From vegetable seeds to gardening tools, fertilizers to gazebos, advertisements should key in on the Financial Positives' love of gardening. The Financial Positives could also be shown enjoying their garden with their grandchildren—another one of their favorite activities.

Financial Positives are committed foreign travelers. They would be attracted to an advertisement for a tour of Italy that shows a traveler drinking a glass of wine, another one of their interests.

In contrast, a promotional package for a Western ski resort to the over-50 market should stress the opportunity to cross-country ski as well as participate in educational seminars. Such an offering would attract the Upbeat Enjoyers and target two of their interests.

In advertising for a comfortable, but stylish line of shoes, a female Upbeat Enjoyer could be shown volunteering as a docent in an art museum. Of all the Self segments, more Upbeat Enjoyers spend time each week in volunteer activities. A quarter of them regularly participate in art and cultural events. Attitudinally, the Upbeat Enjoyers are also the most interested of all the Self segments in wearing clothes that are in style.

**Figure 13–7 Radio Programming Listened to,
50+ Self Segments**

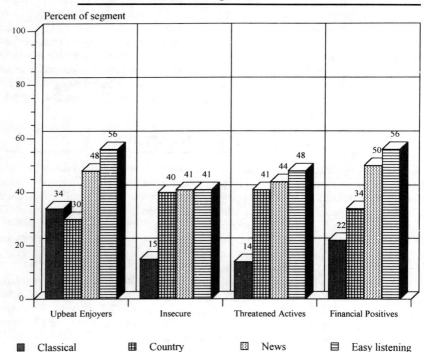

Percent of segment

■ Classical   ⊞ Country   ⊠ News   ⊟ Easy listening

On a multiple-response question listing 11 types of radio programming, more Upbeat Enjoyers and Financial Positives prefer easy listening, while more Insecure and Threatened Actives listen to country. Far more Upbeat Enjoyers favor classical music.

THE DIRECT MAIL OPTION

Correlating attitudes in list purchases

By focusing on behaviors and demographics, the primary parameters in today's databases, direct marketers are limited in their list selection and product development to what is known today, rather than what could be. Targeting a group of people that has never before existed demands a new way of looking at the components of list selection.

Databases for direct marketing can be structured using attitudes that correlate with behaviors and demographics. While we use sophisticated, cutting-edge technologies to find relationships between these various facets, this chapter will indicate how attitudes can be incorporated into the process of selecting and merging and purging a list.

The first question to be answered, however, is how do each of the Self segments react to direct marketing? How good a market are they for such offers?

Financial Positives open direct mail

More Financial Positives (75 percent) are willing to open direct mail and skim its contents as compared to the population over 50 (67 percent). Even greater numbers of male Financial Positives (78 percent) are willing to do so compared to female Financial Positives (72 percent).

Reading contents, keeping direct mail

Females in each Self segment more than males report opening direct mail offers and reading them carefully. For example, more female Threatened Actives (17 percent) read the contents of direct mail carefully than do male Threatened Actives (5 percent) (see Figure 13–8).

Overall, more Insecure (10 percent) put direct mail away to be read later, compared to the over-50 population (8 percent). However, this behavior is higher among female Insecure (12 percent) than male Insecure (5 percent).

Into circular file

Of the over-50 population, 17 percent throw away direct mail unopened. In fact throwing direct mail away unopened is a behavior exhibited by far more males than females in three of the four Self segments. For example, more male Upbeat Enjoyers (21 percent) throw direct mail away unopened as compared to female Upbeat Enjoyers (13 percent). An exception to this behavior is the male Financial Positives subsegment. Only 14 percent of them throw away direct mail unopened.

Turning prospects into customers

Once they have opened a direct mail offer and read its contents, do the Self segments actually order? Compared to the mature population (40 percent), more Financial Positives (46 percent) and Upbeat Enjoyers (43 percent) have ordered something through direct mail in the past three months. The number of Insecure who have ordered is far lower (35 percent).

While 16 percent of the over-50 population have made three or more purchases through direct mail over the past three months, more Upbeat Enjoyers (19 percent) and Financial Positives (18 percent) have done so. Fewer Threatened Actives (11 percent) have made this number of purchases (see Figure 13–9).

Age decreases response rate

For every segment, the percentage who have made a direct mail purchase over the past three months decreases after 65. It is important to note that the decrease is greatest among the Financial Positives (from 52 to 39 percent), but smallest among the Insecure (from 37 to 33 percent).

**Figure 13–8 Opening and Reading Direct Mail,
Males and Females,
65 and Younger and Over 65,
50+ Self Segments**

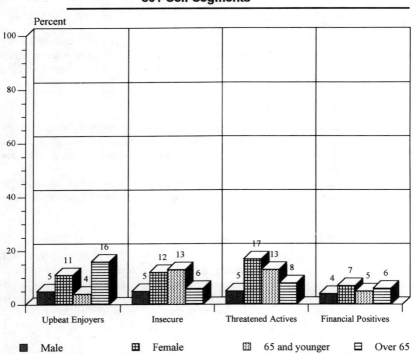

In all segments, more females than males open direct mail and read it carefully. However,
more female Threatened Actives do so as opposed to females in the other segments.
More Insecure and Threatened Actives 65 and younger open direct mail and read it carefully,
while more over-65 Upbeat Enjoyers do so.

Gender another influence

As we have seen, more females as opposed to males in the Self segments are
opening direct mail and reading it carefully. In addition, more females than males in
every segment had made a purchase. For example, while 40 percent of the male
Financial Positives had ordered something through direct mail in the past three months,
50 percent of the females in this segment had done so (see Figure 13–10).

Spending by segment

Not only have more of the Financial Positives made multiple direct mail purchases
over the past three months, but their median expenditures ($70.10) are above that spent

Figure 13–9 Number of Direct Mail Purchases,
50+ Self Segments

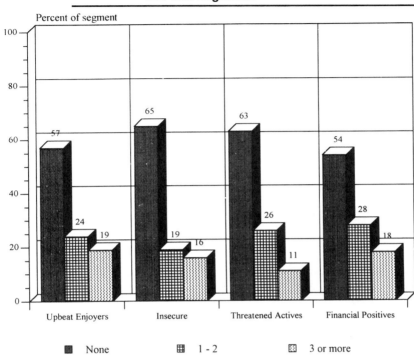

More Financial Positives have made at least one direct mail purchase in the past three months, while slightly more Upbeat Enjoyers have made three or more purchases.

by the over-50 population ($59.83). At $64.18 the Upbeat Enjoyers are second in the amount spent.

Examined by segments and gender, the male Upbeat Enjoyers ($77.56) and female Financial Positives ($77.16) have spent the most on direct mail purchases in the past three months. These figures compare to $59.83 spent by the over-50 population. Although expenditures on direct mail over the past three months by the female Insecure ($56.91) is close to average, the amount spent by the female Upbeat Enjoyers, whose annual income is far higher, is slightly below average ($55.42).

This illustrates the point that opportunities in direct marketing exist not only among those groups with upscale demographic characteristics. Within the direct mail industry, companies targeting lower-income groups have also enjoyed great success.

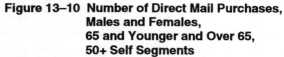

**Figure 13–10 Number of Direct Mail Purchases,
Males and Females,
65 and Younger and Over 65,
50+ Self Segments**

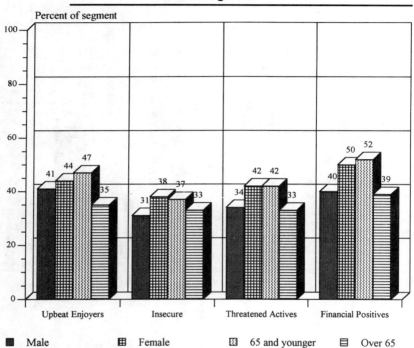

More females and those 65 and younger in all segments have made at least one direct mail purchase in the past three months as opposed to their male and over-65 counterparts. However, more Financial Positives in all subsegments, except males, have made a direct mail purchase in that time.

Age affects expenditures

Although the amount spent on direct mail does decrease with age in each of the Self segments, the difference is greater in some segments than in others. The percent of erosion is greatest between the Financial Positives 65 and younger ($99.60) and those in this segment who are over 65 ($55.22) (see Figure 13–11).

Mature buyers prefer mail

In the realm of direct marketing, more mature consumers use direct mail than phone solicitations or a shopping channel on television. Of the population over 50, more had bought something through direct mail (40 percent) over the past three months compared to purchasing by phone (16 percent) or through a television shopping channel (10 percent).

CREATING TRULY TARGETED MAILING LISTS

Catalog companies such as Land's End, Eddie Bauer, or Orvis that sell clothing or home items through direct mail could target the Upbeat Enjoyers. They are attitudinally the only segment that is predisposed to purchasing through direct mail and also the segment that wants to stay fashionably dressed. A direct marketer wanting to target female Upbeat Enjoyers, 12 percent of the over-50 population, could begin with mailing lists from magazines read by this segment. These publications would include *Family Circle* (32 percent) and *Good Housekeeping* (25 percent).

**Figure 13–11 Median Expenditures on Direct Mail,
65 and Younger and Over 65,
50+ Self Segments**

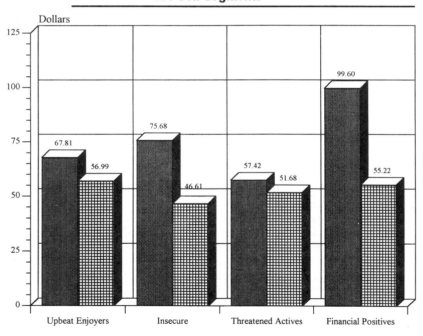

Over the past three months the Financial Positives 65 and younger spent far more on direct mail as compared to the other age-based subsegments. The low-income Insecure 65 and younger were second in expenditures.

Using media, car ownership lists

These lists could be selected by income, sex, and census region, probably the Northeast where 29 percent of the Upbeat Enjoyers live. The list could then be merged and purged using the information below to significantly increase the likelihood of locating female Upbeat Enjoyers.

In looking at car ownership, information that is available from many states, we know that more of the Upbeat Enjoyers drive foreign cars than the other three Self segments. In fact, 5 percent of the female Upbeat Enjoyers own a Honda as their newest car. Of the cars owned by the Upbeat Enjoyers, 27 percent are also 1990 to 1992 models.

Information on credit card use is also available. More female Upbeat Enjoyers (71 percent) have a department store credit card than any other type of card. In fact, far more of them have such a credit card as compared to the population over 50 (53 percent). In addition, this subsegment prefers Visa (44 percent) over American Express (14 percent).

Using such information, marketers can, even on an informal basis, improve their ability to reach those segments who are most interested in their offerings and have the ability to pay. To achieve the greatest success, however, we use statistical methods and cutting-edge technologies such as neural networks and logit analysis to correlate attitudinal segments with demographics and behaviors.

Modeling facilitates targeting

Figure 13-12 shows a "tree diagram" produced by KnowledgeSeeker from FirstMark Technologies in Ottawa. This analysis examines a large battery of demographics and behavioral measures, such as magazine readership in this case, and divides the respondents to focus on meaningful characteristics.

This program examines all of the data and splits the sample to magnify differences between subgroups that are made up of either a high or low percentage of the target segment. Each split is then subdivided, again choosing variables to highlight significant differences expressed in percentages of segment members.

By examining the variables that form the tree, marketers are able to better choose the media with which to communicate to the target segments. For example, while 21 percent of the population over 50 is made up of Threatened Actives, by limiting the selection to males who are high school graduates or less, have incomes below $20,000, and read *Field & Stream,* we increase our probability of reaching the Threatened Actives to 62.5 percent, or another 41.5 percent (see Figure 13–12).

Activities can be mapped

Another type of analysis that would help marketers in list and media selection is seen in Figure 13-13. The map in this figure was produced using a perceptual mapping program called MAPWISE from MarketACTION Research in Peoria, Illinois. This program takes data from a cross-tabulation and presents the relationships in graphic form.

Figure 13-13 shows activities in which the segments regularly participate. The activities shown are those that best correlate with each segment. In interpreting the map, note that when a segment is shown to be close to an activity, it means that this segment participates in the activity at a high level. For example, the Financial Positives are highly involved in personal computers.

Conversely, when a segment and an activity are shown at a distance from one another, the segment participates in that activity at a low level. Thus we can conclude that few Upbeat Enjoyers are involved in hunting and shooting (see Figure 13–13).

CONCLUSION

If considered by individuals and not by households, those over 50 actually consume as much or more than younger persons. Those over 50 are not more or less brand loyal

Figure 13–12 KnowledgeSeeker "Tree Diagram,"
Threatened Actives

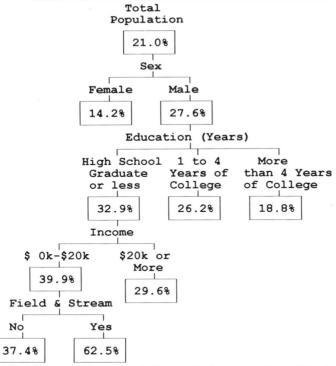

More Threatened Actives can be reached by limiting the selection to males who are high school graduates or less, have incomes under $20,000, and read *Field & Stream*.

than those under 50. Our study shows that brand loyalty is not uniform across all of the 50+ Self segments. By linking a specific attitudinal segment's media and brand preferences, marketers can increase the efficiency of their promotions. The same approach can be applied to the selection of catalogue offerings and list selection.

REFERENCE

Uncles, Mark D., and Andrew S.C. Enrenberg, "Brand Choice among Older Consumers," *Journal of Advertising Research,* August/September 1990, pp. 19-22.

Figure 13–13 Perceptual Map by MAPWISE, 50+ Self Segments

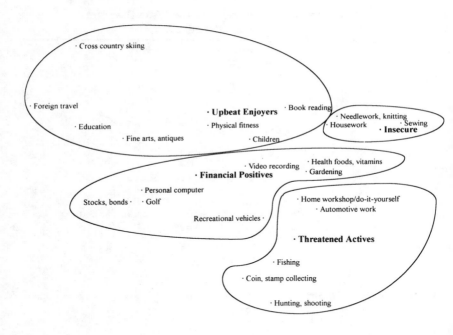

Upbeat Enjoyers are highly involved in physical fitness and book reading compared to the other segments. More Financial Positives selected personal computers as an activity, while more Insecure sew. Threatened Actives, more than the other segments, complete do-it-yourself projects and automotive work.

PART THREE

The Health Segments: Views on Prevention and Sickness

FOURTEEN

THE FOUR HEALTH SEGMENTS

Given the tremendous increase in the number of Americans over 50 in the decades ahead, there will be monumental shifts in how healthcare is paid for and accessibility to that care. Limited resources will increase the number of ethical decisions that physicians, patients, and their families will face.

Motivating consumers to take care of themselves and prevent many diseases will become increasingly more important in reducing our ever-rising healthcare costs. Seeking answers to our healthcare dilemma and the identification of marketing opportunities, we segmented our 50+ respondents based on their attitudes and motivations toward health and healthcare.

In completing our segmentation process, 50 statements were sorted into piles of agreement to disagreement. The statements sorted included:

- At this time of my life, I don't think I can do any more than I am doing to stay healthy.
- Having enough medical insurance is a concern of mine.
- When my doctor gives me medicine, I am very careful to use the entire prescription.
- I actively seek out a great deal of information about how to stay in good health.
- I am careful to eat a balanced diet.
- I believe in getting a yearly physical from my doctor.

Four segments developed from the segmentation methodology described in Chapter 1. These segments are the Proactives, Faithful Patients, Optimists, and Disillusioned.

THE PROACTIVE SEGMENT

The Proactives, 49 percent of the over-50 population, are distinguished by the active role they take in their own healthcare (see Figure 14–1). While working cooperatively with their physicians to stay healthy, the Proactives do their part by

Figure 14–1 Segment Size, 50+ Health Segments

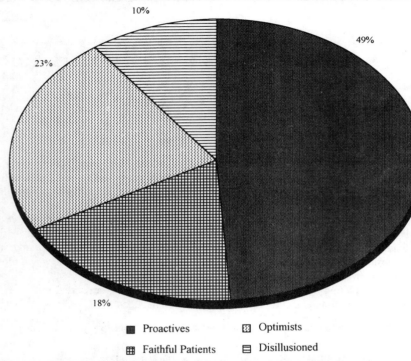

■ Proactives		🔳 Optimists	
⊞ Faithful Patients		🗒 Disillusioned	

The four Health segments include the Proactives (49 percent), the Faithful Patients (18 percent), the Optimists (23 percent), and the Disillusioned (10 percent).

eating nutritious food and exercising. They are quite optimistic that they will stay healthy.

Eating well, exercising

The Proactives don't think they can do any more at this time in their lives than they are already doing to stay healthy. They exercise frequently and believe that they are physically fit. As compared to the other segments, the Proactives would be open to joining a health club just for seniors.

The Proactives are very careful to eat a balanced diet. They are the only segment which agrees that they avoid foods that are high in fat. If any Health segment is "always dieting," it would be the Proactives.

However, the Proactive's preoccupation with their health is a relatively recent development. They agree that as they have grown older, their health has become a greater concern to them. They wish they had eaten a lower fat, more nutritionally balanced diet when they were younger.

Annual physicals important

The Proactives feel much more strongly than do the other segments that they can do something to prevent cancer. However, they admit that they don't understand most of what they hear about this disease.

More than the other segments, Proactives believe in getting an annual physical. They, far more than the other segments, are actively seeking out "a great deal of information about how to stay in good health." When compared with the other segments, the Proactives are the most likely to be considered a "good source of medical information" by their friends.

The Proactives take care of themselves because they wish to continue living. In fact, they are the only Health segment which agrees that they would want to "live as long as they can, even if they are in pain."

Careful about drug use

Proactives also believe that most medicines are beneficial and are not worse than the diseases they treat. They are careful to take an entire prescription. However, the Proactives are the only segment that is concerned about taking over-the-counter drugs and have more of this concern now than when they were younger.

While they place a great deal of faith in medications, they are also careful about those they take. They are the only Health segment that would not, for example, take a drug or medical treatment not approved by the Food and Drug Administration (FDA), even if they thought they needed it.

Hearing aids worth expense

Proactives believe that occasional hearing checks for older people are important and are the only segment which believes that hearing aids are not too expensive for what they do. Nor does this segment believe that a hearing aid makes the wearer look old.

Trust their doctors

Only those in this segment confirm that they are able to find doctors who will listen to them. However, the Proactives wish doctors made house calls. They're the only segment to want this service.

More trusting of doctors than the other segments, the Proactives rely on their doctors' expertise when it comes to knowing about the effects of different medications on older people. If they were having a heart pacemaker implanted, this segment is the least likely to want a second opinion.

Satisfied with insurance

Proactives are the only segment to have confidence that governmental healthcare programs currently in place would provide them with "decent medical care," should they need it. The Proactives feel quite strongly that the medical system is efficient and favor a Health Maintenance Organization (HMO). Only this segment believes that they currently have sufficient medical insurance. They are also the only segment that doesn't blame the high cost of medical insurance on lawyers who sue doctors for "every last little thing that they can find."

DEMOGRAPHICS—THE PROACTIVES

Predominantly female

In comparison to 58 percent of the over-50 population, 60 percent of the Proactives are female (see Figure 14–2).

Oldest Health segment

The oldest of the four Health segments, the Proactives have a median age of 67 years as compared to a median of 64 years for the U.S. population over 50. Twenty-eight percent of those in this segment are age 76 or older as opposed to 23 percent of the over-50 population (see Figure 14–3).

Figure 14–2 Gender, 50+ Health Segments

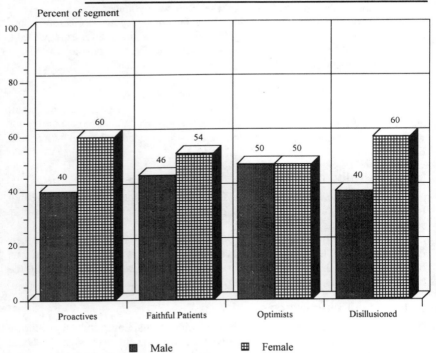

While all other segments have more females than males, only the Optimist segment is equally divided between the sexes.

Most widowed, least divorced

Significantly more of the Proactives (34 percent) are widowed as compared to the U.S. population over 50 (30 percent). However, only 5 percent of the Proactives are divorced or separated. In addition, 56 percent of those in this segment are married. This compares closely to the U.S. population over 50 (58 percent), but is lower than the rate of marriage among the Faithful Patients (66 percent) (see Figure 14–4).

Education level on par

The Proactives have a median of 12 years of education, the same as for the over-50 population. Twenty-five percent of those in this segment have had four years of college or more (see Figure 14–5).

Second lowest income level

Although their median annual pre-tax household income of $27,404 is slightly higher than the median of $25,670 for the U.S. population over 50, the Proactives actually have the second lowest income of the four Health segments. However, more of those in this segment have annual incomes of over $50,000 (25 percent) in comparison to the over-50 population (23 percent). In contrast, only 11 percent of the Disillusioned have incomes this high (see Figure 14–6).

In addition, the Proactives have the second highest level of assets of the four Health segments, a median of $45,938, compared to a median of $43,743 for the over-50 population, excluding their homes. This asset level is far higher than that of the Disillusioned ($20,779), but far lower than that of the Optimists ($67,361).

Living in the South, Midwest

The largest percentage of Proactives (34 percent) resides in the South census region. Another quarter of them live in the Midwest, and 22 percent reside in the Northeast (see Figure 14–7).

Working less

In comparison to 59 percent of the over-50 population and 62 percent of both the Faithful Patients and the Optimists, only 56 percent of the Proactives work either part time or full time (see Figure 14–8).

Professionals before retirement

Over a third of the Proactives have spent their lives employed in white collar jobs. Sixteen percent worked as clericals. Significantly more Proactives (13 percent) are now homemakers or were so before retirement as compared to the over-50 population (10 percent).

Most likely to have retired

The Proactives are the most likely of the four Health segments to have retired. More of those in this segment have retired (55 percent) compared to those over 50 (51 percent), the Faithful Patients (47 percent), and the Disillusioned (46 percent) (see Figure 14–9).

Least likely to return to work

The Proactives, along with the Faithful Patients, are the least likely of the Health segments to be employed after retiring. Of those Proactives who have retired, a quarter have returned to work, the lowest percentage of the Health segments (see Figure 14–9). In comparison, 29 percent of the over-50 population have retired and returned to work.

Figure 14–3 Age, 50+ Health Segments

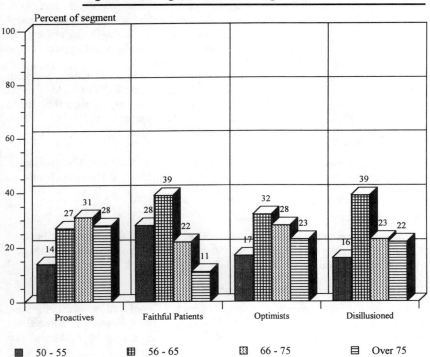

Compared to the other segments, far more Faithful Patients are in the 50-55 age group, while far more Proactives are in the over-75 category.

Return to professional, clerical work

Of the quarter of the Proactives who returned to work after retirement, most took white collar jobs (25 percent). In addition, 11 percent became employed in clerical positions.

Volunteering more

This segment is more likely to volunteer than the other Health segments. Of the Proactives, 52 percent volunteer their time as opposed to only 45 percent of the U.S. population over 50 and about one-third of each of the Disillusioned and Faithful Patients.

Demographic summary

The Proactives are the oldest and the most widowed of the four Health segments. They have a median of 12 years of education and a median annual household income of $27,404, the second lowest of these segments. However, they have the second highest level of assets. More Proactives live in the South than in any other region.

Those in this segment, most of whom work or did work in professional or technical and clerical positions, are the most likely of the four Health segments to retire and the least likely to be employed after retiring. In comparison to the over-50 population, fewer Proactives work either part time or full time. However, far more of the Proactives volunteer their time.

THE FAITHFUL PATIENT SEGMENT

Our attitudinal segmentation shows that the second segment, the Faithful Patients, are characterized by a trust in and dependence on the medical system and in medication. The Faithful Patients are 18 percent of the population over 50 (see Figure 14–1).

Doing little for health

Although Faithful Patients are aware that they should eat well and exercise to stay healthy, they do not believe they are doing all they can in this regard. Of all the segments, the Faithful Patients believe they aren't getting enough exercise to remain physically fit. While they wish that they had taken more care to eat a balanced diet and less fat when they were younger, they are still the segment least likely to be eating a balanced diet in the present. This segment denies that it is always dieting.

Much more than the other segments, the Faithful Patients are more concerned about their health now than when they were younger. However, they agree that they do little to improve it.

Physicals important

With greater intensity than the other segments, the Faithful Patients believe it's important to have their hearing checked and get yearly physicals.

Don't want to live in pain

In contrast to the Proactive segment, the Faithful Patients, along with the Optimists and Disillusioned, do not wish to live as long as they can if they are in pain.

Using OTC, generic drugs

The Faithful Patients agree that they only take medicine when it is "absolutely necessary." However, they agree with this statement at a far lower level than do the Disillusioned or the Optimists, the segment that is adamant on this point. In contrast to the other segments, the Faithful Patients are the most likely to continually try new over-the-counter (OTC) drugs to make themselves feel better. Of all the Health segments, they are also the ones who are most likely to rely on their pharmacist to recommend OTC drugs.

While they have the highest level of agreement with the idea that most medicines are worthwhile, the Faithful Patients don't rely on specific brands of prescription drugs. The Faithful Patients are, in fact, the only segment to prefer generic drugs over those with brand names. More than the other segments, the Faithful Patients agree that taking medicines is better than having the disease. The Faithful Patients are compliant patients, careful to use an entire prescription.

Rely on doctors, specialists

Besides their strong faith in medications, the Faithful Patients also trust their doctors. Regardless of their faith in physicians, however, the Faithful Patients would seek a second opinion if a doctor recommended that they have a heart pacemaker implanted. The doctors they prefer are specialists. For example, they think it's better to have their eyes checked by an ophthalmologist than by an optometrist.

The Faithful Patients are open to radical treatments. They would consider eye surgery if they were sure it would improve their eyesight. Besides their faith in physicians and in medications, the Faithful Patients are, interestingly enough, the only segment that "turns to religion" in times of poor health.

Health insurance adequate

Although concerned about having enough medical insurance, the Faithful Patients do believe they have medical insurance adequate for any medical problem.

Negative on healthcare delivery system

The Faithful Patients don't believe there are any government programs that would provide them with "decent medical care." Lawsuits with lawyers suing doctors "for every last little thing" are to blame for the high cost of health insurance. This segment favors HMOs.

DEMOGRAPHICS—THE FAITHFUL PATIENTS

Fewer females than over-50 population

In comparison to 58 percent of the U.S. population over 50, only 54 percent of the Faithful Patients are female (see Figure 14–2).

Youngest Health segment

With a median age of 60 years, the Faithful Patients are the youngest of the four Health segments. In comparison to only 18 percent of the over-50 population, 28 percent of the Faithful Patients are between the ages of 50 and 55. On the other hand, only 11 percent of the Faithful Patients are 76 or older, as opposed to 23 percent of the over-50 population. In contrast, 28 percent of the Proactives are in that age group (see Figure 14–3).

Most married, least widowed

The Faithful Patients are the most married of the Health segments at 66 percent, compared to 58 percent of the over-50 population. In addition, fewer Faithful Patients (21 percent) are widowed as compared to the U.S. population over 50 (30 percent). One-third of the Disillusioned and the Proactives are widowed (see Figure 14–4).

Highly educated

With a median of 13 years of education, the Faithful Patients, along with the Optimists, are the most highly educated of the Health segments. In comparison to 26 percent of the over-50 population, more of the Faithful Patients (28 percent) have attended four years of college or more (see Figure 14–5).

Finances not a concern

The Faithful Patients have a median annual pre-tax household income of $32,333, only about $100 less than that of the Optimists, who have the highest income of the four Health segments. Among the Health segments, however, the Faithful Patients have the highest percentage (29 percent) of seniors with incomes of $50,000 or more, significantly higher than those in the U.S. population over 50 with this income level (23 percent) (see Figure 14–6).

On the other hand, the Faithful Patients have the second lowest level of assets of the four Health segments, a median of $45,203, excluding their homes. This asset level is slightly above that of the U.S. population over 50 ($43,743) and far higher than that of the Disillusioned ($20,779).

Southern living

Like all the Health segments, more Faithful Patients (37 percent) live in the South than in any other census region. In addition, there are more Faithful Patients than any other segment in the South. Almost a quarter of the Faithful Patients reside in the Northeast and in the Midwest (see Figure 14–7).

Figure 14–4 Marital Status, 50+ Health Segments

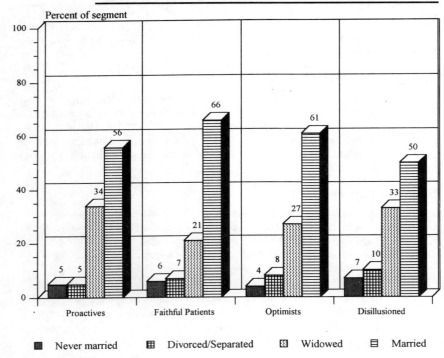

Compared to the other segments, more of the Faithful Patients are married. More of the Proactives and Disillusioned are widowed. The Disillusioned are also the most divorced or separated of the segments.

Saying "yes" to work

The Faithful Patients, along with the Optimists, do more paid work than the other Health segments. More Faithful Patients (62 percent) work at either part-time or full-time jobs as compared to the over-50 population (59 percent), the Disillusioned (56 percent), and the Proactives (56 percent) (see Figure 14–8).

More professionals and clericals

Twenty-five percent of the Faithful Patients had careers in professional or technical positions. Of the Faithful Patients, 16 percent were clerical workers. Fourteen percent spent their lives working as managers or executives. In addition, in comparison to the over-50 population as a whole, significantly more Faithful Patients were laborers before retiring.

Figure 14–5 Level of Education, 50+ Health Segments

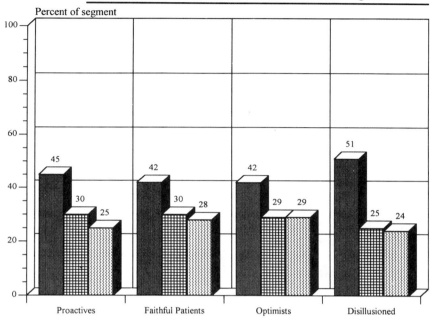

High school graduate or less ⊞ Some college/technical school
🔲 4 - year college degree or more

The Disillusioned are the least educated of the Health segments; more Faithful Patients and Optimists have a 4-year college degree or more.

Not looking to retire

In comparison to 51 percent of the over-50 population and 55 percent of the Proactives, fewer of the Faithful Patients (47 percent) have retired with no intention of returning to work (see Figure 14–9).

Few employed after retirement

Of those Faithful Patients who have retired, only 25 percent have been employed since taking their retirement, compared to 29 percent of the over-50 population. Far more of the Optimists (35 percent) and Disillusioned (41 percent) have retired and returned to work (see Figure 14–9).

Homemakers, professionals, clericals after retirement

When returning to work after retirement, 23 percent of the Faithful Patients became homemakers. Seventeen percent took professional or technical positions and 14 percent became clerical workers.

Least likely to volunteer

Of all the Health segments, the Faithful Patients are the least likely to spend their time volunteering. Only 34 percent of the Faithful Patients, in comparison to 45 percent of the U.S. population over 50 and 52 percent of the Proactives, do volunteer work.

Demographic summary

The youngest of the four Health segments, the Faithful Patients are the most married and the least widowed. They, along with the Optimists, are one of the two most highly educated Health segments. The Faithful Patients have the second highest income of the Health segments, only slightly below that of the Optimists, but the second lowest level of assets. More Faithful Patients live in the South than in any other region.

The Faithful Patients, most of whom had careers in professional or clerical positions, are less likely to have retired and less likely to be employed after retirement than the U.S. population over 50. More of the Faithful Patients, as compared to those over 50, work for pay either full time or part time, although fewer do volunteer work.

THE OPTIMIST SEGMENT

The third Health segment, the Optimists, comprises 23 percent of the population over 50 (see Figure 14–1). They consider themselves to be healthy and are upbeat about staying that way. Blessed with either great genes or good luck, the Optimists do little to maintain their health.

Optimistic about health

Optimists feel that they almost never get sick. They're the only segment to agree with this statement, and they do so at a high level. In addition, although they and the Proactives believe that they are "optimistic about staying in good health," the Optimists believe this statement with greater intensity.

Perhaps because they aren't getting sick now and believe they will stay in good health, the Optimists aren't interested in living as long as they can if it involves living in pain.

Satisfied with fitness level

The Optimists, who believe they are getting enough exercise to maintain good fitness, wouldn't join a health club just for seniors.

Of the four segments, only the Optimists don't wish they had eaten a diet lower in fat and more nutritionally balanced when they were younger. Neither are the Optimists "always on a diet."

Enjoying life

Optimists live life to the fullest now and don't worry about a long life. They feel that if they are going to get cancer, they'll get it whatever they do. However, Optimists exercise and feel they are doing all they can to stay healthy.

Focused on enjoying life, rather than espousing healthcare trends, it isn't surprising that the Optimists' friends don't consider them to be "good sources of medical information."

Putting off hearing checks

While the Optimists don't believe hearing aids make the wearer look old, they don't reveal an interest in having their hearing checked occasionally.

Cautious with drugs

For the Optimists, reliance on drugs, whether prescription or over-the-counter, isn't at the forefront of their health concerns. There are only two drug-related statements toward which the Optimists exhibit strong feelings. This segment, far more than the others, takes medicine only when it is absolutely necessary. They will also not try new over-the-counter drugs in order to feel better.

Prefer specialists

The Optimists generally trust doctors. Given their negative views of lawsuit-prone lawyers driving up health insurance costs, it is in character that they would not sue a doctor who made a mistake while treating them. However, their level of trust in physicians is somewhat lower than that of the Proactives and the Faithful Patients. For example, the Optimists, along with the Faithful Patients and the Disillusioned, would get a second opinion if a doctor recommended getting a pacemaker.

They do believe in the benefits of going to specialists and would prefer having their eyes checked by an ophthalmologist over an optometrist. They would also have surgery to improve their eyesight. Interestingly enough, the Optimists are the only Health segment that does not believe in getting a yearly physical.

Adequate insurance a concern

Optimists feel very strongly that the United States does not need guaranteed healthcare. However, they are quite convinced that government programs do not currently exist that would provide medical care if they needed it. The Optimists are concerned about having enough medical insurance and they blame lawyers for its high cost. The Optimists are the only segment that doesn't believe HMOs are a good idea.

DEMOGRAPHICS—THE OPTIMISTS

Half females, half males

Evenly divided between males and females, the Optimist segment has significantly more males than the over-50 population (43 percent) or any other Health segment (see Figure 14–2).

Figure 14–6 Annual Pre-Tax Household Income, 50+ Health Segments

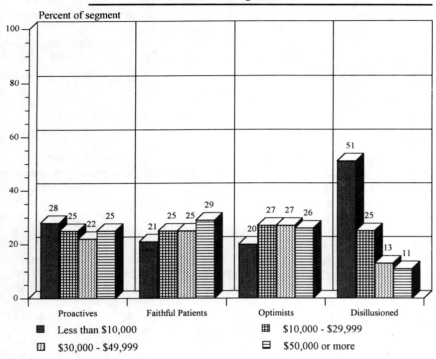

Percent of segment

	Proactives	Faithful Patients	Optimists	Disillusioned

■ Less than $10,000   ⊞ $10,000 - $29,999

▩ $30,000 - $49,999   ⊟ $50,000 or more

More Disillusioned have annual pre-tax household incomes of less than $10,000. In contrast, more Faithful Patients have incomes of $50,000 or more.

Second oldest segment

The Optimists are the second oldest Health segment with a median age of 65 years. Half the Optimists (51 percent) are 66 or older (see Figure 14–3).

Higher marriage rate than norm

Of those in this segment, 61 percent are married, significantly more than the 58 percent of the over-50 population. In contrast, only 50 percent of the Disillusioned are married (see Figure 14–4).

Most highly educated

With a median of 13 years of education, the Optimists and the Faithful Patients are the most highly educated of the Health Segments. In comparison to 26 percent of all those over 50, 29 percent of the Optimists have attended four years of college or more (see Figure 14–5).

Wealthiest Health segment

The wealthiest of the four Health segments, the Optimists have a median annual pre-tax household income of $32,430, only slightly higher than the Faithful Patients' median income of $32,333. Twenty-six percent of those in this segment have incomes of $50,000 or more, significantly more than the 23 percent of the over-50 population with incomes at this level (see Figure 14–6).

In addition, of the four Health segments, the Optimists have the highest level of assets, excluding their homes. Their median level of assets ($67,361) is far higher than that of the U.S. population over 50 ($43,743) and in dramatic contrast to that of the Disillusioned ($20,779).

Figure 14–7 Residence within Census Regions, 50+ Health Segments

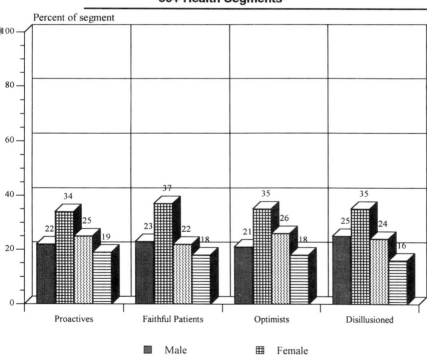

More of all of the Health segments live in the South than in any other region. Compared to the other three segments, however, more Faithful Patients reside in the South, more Optimists in the Midwest, and more Disillusioned in the Northeast.

Southern and Midwestern living

The Optimists are most heavily concentrated in the South (35 percent) and Midwest (26 percent) census regions. Twenty-one percent of the Optimists live in the Northeast and 18 percent live in the West (see Figure 14–7).

Majority are working

Compared to 40 percent of the over-50 population, 62 percent of the Optimists work either part time or full time (see Figure 14–8).

Professionals and managers

Significantly more Optimists, as compared to the over-50 population, made careers for themselves in professional or technical (29 percent as compared to 24 percent),

Figure 14–8 Hours of Paid Employment Per Week, 50+ Health Segments

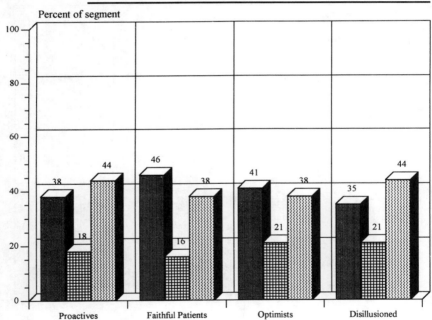

■ 35 hours a week or more   ⊞ Fewer than 35 hours a week   ▨ Zero hours

More Faithful Patients and Optimists work full time. Fewer Proactives and Disillusioned work for pay.

managerial or executive (15 percent as compared to 12 percent), and owner or entrepreneur (10 percent as compared to 8 percent) positions.

Majority are retiring

Fifty-two percent of the Optimists have retired with the intention of never returning to work, paralleling the 51 percent of the over-50 population that has done so (see Figure 14–9).

More Optimists returning to work

Compared to only 29 percent of all those over 50, 35 percent of those Optimists who have retired have been employed since their retirement (see Figure 14–9).

Wide range of positions after retirement

Of those Optimists who returned to work after retirement, 21 percent became homemakers, 18 percent took professional or technical positions, 9 percent became owners or entrepreneurs, and 8 percent took sales jobs.

Volunteering on par

More of the Optimists (48 percent) volunteer their time as compared to the over-50 population (45 percent), the Disillusioned (36 percent), or the Faithful Patients (34 percent).

Demographic summary

Made up of equal percentages of males and females, the Optimist segment is the second oldest of the four Health segments. More of the Optimists, as compared to the over-50 population, are married. Those in this segment are the wealthiest in terms of both income and assets, although their income level is only slightly above that of the Faithful Patients. This segment is also one of two of the most highly educated of the Health segments. Most Optimists reside in the South and the Midwest.

Fifty-two percent of those in this segment have retired, while 35 percent have returned to work since taking retirement. These percentages are similar to those for the U.S. population over 50. More of the Optimists, who made careers as professionals, managers, and entrepreneurs, work for pay, as opposed to the over-50 population. However, their level of volunteer work is on par with the percentage of all those over 50 who volunteer.

THE DISILLUSIONED SEGMENT

We've labeled the last Health segment the Disillusioned. At 10 percent of the over-50 population, the Disillusioned are characterized by their lack of faith in the medical system, and their strong desire for better medical insurance coverage in the United States (see Figure 14–1).

Want to live long, healthy lives

The Disillusioned are willing to take a somewhat active role in their own well-being. They believe in getting a yearly physical examination. They also actively seek out information about how to stay healthy and believe they can do things to prevent cancer. The Disillusioned are careful to eat a balanced diet.

In direct contrast to the Optimists, the Disillusioned are worried about living a long life. However, they wouldn't wish to live such a life if it meant living in pain.

Distrust doctors

The Disillusioned are the least trusting of doctors. They are the only segment which fears that physicians don't know enough about how different medicines interact when taken by older people. If a doctor recommended a heart pacemaker, they would get a second opinion. But although they distrust the system, the Disillusioned would not sue a doctor who made a mistake in treating them.

Conservative drug use

The Disillusioned take medications only when it is absolutely necessary. They aren't always trying new over-the-counter drugs in order to feel better.

Attractive eyeglasses important

While the Disillusioned have the least concern of any of the segments that hearing aids make the wearer look old, they do care about the attractiveness of their eyeglass frames. Sturdiness isn't enough.

Support guaranteed healthcare

The Disillusioned are very concerned about having enough medical insurance. They disagree very strongly that their insurance is adequate to cover any medical problem. While they think that HMOs are a good idea, the Disillusioned are adamant that the United States should have guaranteed healthcare for all its citizens.

The statement on guaranteed healthcare for all is the one that this segment agrees with most intensely. This segment, concerned about their own inadequate coverage, views the medical system as expensive because it is inefficient.

DEMOGRAPHICS—THE DISILLUSIONED

Predominantly women

Sixty percent of the Disillusioned, compared to 58 percent of the U.S. population over 50, are women. In contrast, only 50 percent of the Optimists are women (see Figure 14–2).